SUCCESS IN CIRCUIT LIES

DIDEROT'S
COMMUNICATIONAL PRACTICE

Tell all the Truth but tell it slant —
Success in Circuit lies.
EMILY DICKINSON

What a singular thing conversation is . . .
Look at the circuits we have taken.
DIDEROT
"LETTRES À SOPHIE VOLLAND"

SUCCESS IN CIRCUIT LIES

DIDEROT'S COMMUNICATIONAL PRACTICE

ROSALINA DE LA CARRERA

STANFORD UNIVERSITY PRESS
STANFORD, CALIFORNIA

1991

Stanford University Press
Stanford, California
© 1991 by the Board of Trustees
of the Leland Stanford Junior University
Printed in the United States of America

Published with the assistance of Amherst College

CIP data are at the end of the book

For Wilda Anderson
and
François and Jacqueline Roustang

ACKNOWLEDGMENTS

I would like, above all, to thank Wilda Anderson, who throughout the writing of this book offered endless encouragement, support, and editorial advice. Each and every page that follows was improved by the revisions she suggested; each and every day I spent writing was brightened by her steadfast friendship and concern.

I'll never forget the day François Roustang searched through the stacks of the Johns Hopkins library with me, as we both tried to locate a passage from the *Correspondance littéraire* in the hope that it would confirm one of my hunches about *La Religieuse*. From that moment on, he took an active interest in my project that inspired me to keep on going even when I wanted to stop. I thank him here for all the encouragement he has given me over the years.

My sincere gratitude goes to the many friends and colleagues who read the manuscript and provided helpful suggestions: Josué Harari, always an exacting and perceptive reader; Marie-Hélène Huet and Jay Caplan, generous intellectual interlocutors; Michael Fried, from whom I learned so much about Diderot. I am also deeply grateful to Thomas Kavanagh and Walter E. Rex for their many insightful comments and for their support.

Several members of the Amherst College community have made an enormous difference: Stephanie Sandler has seen me through thick and thin since my first days at Amherst; Richard Fink has been unwavering in his support; Thomas Dumm and Brenda Bright have challenged me to rethink many assumptions; Antonio Benítez Rojo and Hilda Otaño Benítez have brought me closer to my cultural and intellectual roots during many evenings spent talking about Cuba, about literature, and about everything else under the sun.

I am also indebted to Virginia DuCharme, administrative assistant *extraordinaire*, whose intelligence, patience, and warmth work magic every day in the Department of Romance Languages at Amherst.

Margaret Groesbeck and Michael Kasper were indefatigable in their efforts to help me locate sources and check bibliographical references. I thank them not just for their assistance in doing my research but also for their boundless sense of fun.

Many thanks to my wonderful editor, Helen Tartar, for her enthusiasm (which never flagged) and her help (which she always so unstintingly gave). My thanks also to John Ziemer, word-sculptor, for the elegance with which he chiseled away the rough contours of sentences and paragraphs, and for his remarkable patience in answering my questions.

Finally, I would like to express my gratitude to the American Council of Learned Societies and to Amherst College for fellowships that made possible the completion of this book.

A shorter version of Chapter 2 originally appeared in *The Eighteenth Century: Theory and Interpretation*, and I am grateful to the editors for permission to use this material here.

One last word of thanks: to Larry Bassett, for having understood why we couldn't leave for New Mexico any sooner than we did.

R.d.l.C.

CONTENTS

CHAPTER ONE
INTRODUCTION
3

CHAPTER TWO
EPISTOLARY DECOYS
INDIRECT COMMUNICATION IN THE "PRÉFACE-ANNEXE" OF "LA RELIGIEUSE"
11

CHAPTER THREE
MUSICAL CONVERSATIONS
NARRATIVE MODELS AND COMMUNICATION IN "LA RELIGIEUSE"
41

CHAPTER FOUR

DETOURS THROUGH TIME AND SPACE
DIDEROT'S LATE HISTORICAL WRITINGS

83

CHAPTER FIVE

PRELIMINARY DISCOURSES
NATURAL PHILOSOPHY IN D'ALEMBERT'S BOUDOIR

127

CHAPTER SIX

CONCLUSION

169

APPENDIX

THE "PRÉFACE-ANNEXE" OF "LA RELIGIEUSE"

179

NOTES

213

INDEX

231

SUCCESS IN CIRCUIT LIES

DIDEROT'S
COMMUNICATIONAL PRACTICE

CHAPTER ONE

INTRODUCTION

All sorts of impressions are made, but our attention focuses only on one. The soul in the midst of its sensations is like a guest at a tumultuous table who speaks to his neighbor and does not hear the others.

— Diderot, *Eléments de physiologie*

The twentieth century has lately been rediscovering the roots of its modernity in the eighteenth century. Starting with Derrida's rereading of Rousseau, contemporary critics have been exploring the intellectual affinities that bind the two centuries. Although much of their attention has focused on Rousseau, several recent studies have been devoted to establishing the modernity of Diderot.[1]

Interestingly, two of these studies have seen Diderot's approach to the problem of order and disorder as one of the principal links between his age and ours.[2]

From Diderot's perspective, order and disorder, which according to traditional rationalist definitions are mutually exclusive categories, function instead as mutually generative phenomena. Diderot bases this conclusion on his view of the workings of nature, in which disorder produces order, which in turn produces disorder, and so forth. It is the continual shift from the one to the other that constitutes nature's creative process.

Modern scientists and theorists of science have come to similar conclusions about the workings of nature.[3] Diderot's notion of the creative role of order and disorder in the natural world resonates strongly not only with that of modern scientific theorists but also with that of contemporary philosophers of science.[4] It is in these resonances that the present study has its own roots. Its main focus, however, is neither the problem of Diderot's modernity as such nor the larger issue of order and disorder, but communication, which for Diderot is a corollary of the problem of order and disorder. This premise makes sense, however, only when one takes into consideration the specific characteristics of communication as Diderot defines them in the *Rêve de d'Alembert*. This text clearly demonstrates that Diderotian communication is a material process and as such follows the same laws as other processes in the natural world. Hence Diderot's conclusion that disorder is an integral part of the process of communication.

Modern scientific theorists are still attempting to come to terms with the question of the role of disorder in nature. In his work on thermodynamics, for example, Ilya Prigogine, the Nobel Prize–winning chemist, argues that disorder can produce forms of order in the natural world. His claim is that irreversible processes, long held to have nothing but destructive effects, can, under certain circumstances, take on a constructive role and generate forms of order. Specifically, in systems maintained far from their point of equilibrium, random fluctuations occurring at the microscopic level can amplify themselves and affect the whole system, thereby becoming the source of new, orderly formations at the macroscopic level. These new structures eventually will dissipate, only to create the possibility of orderly formations of a new kind.[5]

A similar process takes place in living organisms, which are prototypes of the "dissipative structures" Prigogine describes, for organisms use aleatory events (or disorder) as integral components of their organization. This apparently contradictory logic, which calls into question the classical opposition between the terms "random" (or "disorderly") and "organized," has been most clearly formulated by the biophysicist Henri Atlan.[6] Atlan argues that organisms are able to counter the potentially perturbatory effects of random, unpredictable events in their surroundings—events which for them at first constitute environmental disorder or "noise," disorder's analogue in information theory—by modifying their structures and reorganizing at a higher level of complexity. Atlan calls this the "complexity from noise" principle. It is important to note, however, that the increased complexity of an organism that has undergone the process Atlan describes does not imply its superiority, since complexity is a function of what the observer *does not know* about the living system he is observing and not of the system's inherent properties. As one analyst has summarized Atlan's views, his notions of order and complexity

> do not make sense unless one considers that they characterize a way of knowing natural organized beings, and not the properties intrinsic to them, which, in their possible determinations, are inaccessible both by definition and situation to *total* knowledge on the part of the observer. . . . It is in this context that the organizing role of chance can be understood. Chance, "noise," reduces the constraints that organize the system for the observer. The latter is therefore able to diagnose an increase in variety, which is to say, again, an increase *for him*—let us not forget this—in "disorder." But as the system hypothetically continues to be organized and to function, the observer is forced to postulate that chance has been converted into new meanings for the system, meanings to which he, the observer, has no access.[7]

Nevertheless, according to Atlan the increase in a given organism's complexity does have a positive functional role, since it augments that organism's potential for future adaptation to other random events in its environment.

It is in the context of these theories of the role of disorder in various domains of the natural world that we can situate Michel Serres's work on communication. Generalizing from the findings of communications engineers who in the mid-twentieth century discovered that shocks occurring on the molecular level in the material components of electronic systems invariably produced static or noise, noise that the engineers were able to reduce but found impossible to eliminate, Serres argues that all forms of communication—and not just technological ones—possess a characteristic "pathology." Written modes of communication are characterized by illegible handwriting, typographical errors, and misspellings; in spoken communication interference may be created by stuttering, regional accents, or mispronunciations. From a positivistic perspective, which postulates the possibility of clear and transparent transmission of messages, these various "pathologies" would be deemed obstacles to communication.[8] From Serres's perspective, however, they take on an altogether different cast. Serres claims that noise (the term he chooses to designate the totality of the pathologies) not only does not constitute an obstacle to communication but is instead the very factor that allows communication to take place.[9]

Serres argues, in the first instance, that noise is necessary to the constitution of a message. In the same way that positive and negative spaces in drawing and painting can be defined only in terms of each other, since negative space is the background from which positive space emerges, so a message takes shape only against a background of noise. The same logic enters into Serres's redefinition of dialogue, in which he explains why noise is the factor that allows messages to be exchanged between two interlocutors.

> [A dialogue] is a sort of game played by two interlocutors considered as united against the phenomena of interference and confusion, or against individuals with some stake in interrupting communication. These interlocutors are in no way opposed, as in the traditional conception of the dialectic game; on the contrary, they are on the same side, tied together by a mutual inter-

est: they battle together against noise. . . . *To hold a dialogue is to suppose a third man and to seek to exclude him*; a successful communication is the exclusion of the third man.¹⁰

On the one hand, the intrusion of noise into a circuit of communication between two interlocutors threatens to disrupt the exchange. On the other hand, however, it is this very threat that ultimately allows communication to take place, since it creates a bond between the two interlocutors; instead of maintaining an adversary relationship, they join forces to block out the noise that could potentially interrupt their exchange. The inclusion (and subsequent exclusion) of noise as a third term in any exchange between two interlocutors leads Serres to substitute a ternary model of dialogue for the traditional binary one.

I needed an approach that would allow me to begin to talk not just about the thematic links between Diderot's views of communication and those of contemporary theorists but also about the more textually specific analogies. Here Serres's theories proved useful as a heuristic device, allowing me to identify specific instances of Diderot's use of ternary communicational models. As my work progressed, however, I found that there were as many differences as similarities between Diderot's model of communication and Serres's. Though there continued to be aspects of Diderot's ternary model that had analogies in Serres's—analogies that I shall have occasion to point out as we go along—I discovered nevertheless that Diderot's writings themselves generate a ternary model of communication that is uniquely his.

Strangely enough, the locus of this discovery was the *Préface-annexe* of *La Religieuse*, one of Diderot's most puzzling and frequently controversial texts. Although the *Préface-annexe* was long held to be an account of the actual historical events that led Diderot to write *La Religieuse*, Herbert Dieckmann's famous analysis of the autograph manuscript of the *Préface-annexe*, published in 1952, demonstrated that Diderot meant this text to be just as much a fiction as the rest of *La Religieuse*.[11] Dieckmann's findings opened the way for the kind of reading I propose to do in the present study, a reading that analyzes the *Préface-annexe*'s literary devices as a willful construction and not as a historical account.*

It is through a detailed textual analysis of the *Préface-annexe* of *La Religieuse* that I extract Diderot's own idiosyncratic model of communication. I shall then trace this model through a series of texts drawn from the domains of fiction (the rest of *La Religieuse* and *Jacques le fataliste*), history (the *Histoire des Deux Indes* and the *Essai sur les règnes de Claude et de Néron*), and natural philosophy (the *Rêve de d'Alembert*), identifying the particular uses to which Diderot puts his communicational model in each of these contexts.

I have tried to describe in as much detail as possible the specific mechanisms that Diderot uses to structure the relationship between text and reader, and to bring the unique characteristics of those mechanisms into focus. I hope that my study will ultimately provide a new perspective from which to view Diderot's communicational practice, not just as it appears in the texts I have chosen to examine but throughout the entire corpus of his writings.

*For a translation of the *Préface-annexe*, see the Appendix, pp. 179–209. If I may borrow a tactic from Diderot, I would urge readers to read the Appendix first.

CHAPTER TWO

EPISTOLARY DECOYS

INDIRECT COMMUNICATION
IN THE "PRÉFACE-ANNEXE"
OF "LA RELIGIEUSE"

An epistolary exchange is, traditionally, a binary process, consisting of letters sent by one person directly to another, who in turn replies. The *Préface-annexe* of *La Religieuse* appears to satisfy the preceding definition, since it contains the texts of the letters exchanged between the Marquis de Croismare and Diderot alias Suzanne Saulier, called Simonin. These letters, so the story goes, were part of an elaborate plot Diderot and some friends concocted to entice the Marquis into returning to Paris from his self-imposed exile at his country estate near Caen.[1] Knowing that the Marquis's imagination had once been captivated by the case of a nun who was suing to have her vows annulled — to the point where he had personally intervened on her behalf in the Paris Parlement — the conspirators had concluded that they could trick the Marquis into returning to Paris by making him believe the same nun had now escaped from her convent and needed his help. Hence the epistolary exchange, as Suzanne writes to the Marquis asking for his assistance, or so Grimm tells us in his narrative from the *Correspondance littéraire*, which frames the letters and in which he recounts the events of the plot.[2]

But is this an epistolary exchange in the conventional sense?

Shortly after Grimm's assertion that Diderot wrote to the Marquis in Suzanne's name asking for his help and protection, the text of Suzanne's first letter to the Marquis appears. But curiously, when Suzanne wants to get in touch with the Marquis, she sends her letter not to him but to his cousin, the Comte de Croismare, at an address in Paris: "Note from the nun to Monsieur the *Comte* de Croismare, Governor of the Royal Military School" (my emphasis).³ Only after she receives the Marquis's cousin's reply informing her that the person she seeks is currently residing in Caen does Suzanne write to the Marquis. Similarly, one could assume that when the Marquis wants to answer Suzanne's letter, he will write directly to her at her address in Paris. Instead, the Marquis's first reply is addressed to Madame Madin in Versailles. And despite Grimm's assurances that the correspondence he reproduces in the *Préface-annexe* took place between Diderot alias Suzanne and the Marquis de Croismare, an inventory of the letters reveals that in fact thirteen of the twenty letters are exchanged between Madame Madin and the Marquis, and not between the nun and the Marquis.

If we now reconsider the definition of an epistolary exchange with which we began, we find that much in the structure of the correspondence between the Marquis and Suzanne in the *Préface-annexe* invalidates the definition of an epistolary exchange as a binary process, suggesting instead that it is a ternary process.⁴ Rather than presupposing that two correspondents are sufficient to initiate and successfully maintain an exchange of letters, Diderot's model requires that there be a minimum of three. Consistently, the various forms of communication in Diderot's novels seem to take an indirect rather than a direct path. The most explicit example of this aspect of Diderot's texts is embodied in the *Préface-annexe*, which makes this the ideal text to use to explore Diderot's model of indirect communication. The very premise of the plot of the *Préface-*

annexe relies on a ternary structure. Suzanne is the third party who will provoke the Marquis to leave Caen and return to Paris. Never does the thought seem to cross the mind of the conspirators that they could write directly to the Marquis, tell him that he is sorely missed, and achieve the results they seek.

If successful communication in the *Préface-annexe* must be indirect and ternary, then why does Suzanne's first letter to the Marquis, which she sends directly to him, elicit a favorable response from him? The letter itself, read in conjunction with the section of Grimm's narrative that precedes it, suggests an answer. From the beginning of her letter, Suzanne gives broad hints that she has already been in contact with someone *else* — the Marquis's cousin, the Comte. The purpose of these hints, obviously, is to plant the suggestion in the Marquis's mind that he should investigate the matter with his cousin, thus initiating an exchange between them on the subject of Suzanne, her letter, her problems, and so forth. Suzanne's first letter establishes, therefore, the necessity of a third party (outside the circuit of communication) through whom information about her can be conveyed indirectly.

Diderot and the conspirators, furthermore, apparently had already foreseen the interesting possibilities posed by the letter sent to the Comte for conveying information about Suzanne to the Marquis by indirect means, except they had imagined that the Comte would be the one to initiate the exchange. "There also existed the possibility that the governor of the Royal Military School would tease his cousin about the note and send it to him, which would give an air of great authenticity to our virtuous adventurer" (34). The comments included in Suzanne's letter to the Marquis about her inquiries at the Royal Military School seem designed to ensure that from one angle or another, the Comte and the Marquis will be motivated to discuss Suzanne.

Suzanne's letter, moreover, opens the circuit of communication not only to the indirect participation of the Marquis's cousin, but also to the indirect participation of another party, who goes under the name of Madame Madin. In her first letter, Suzanne introduces Madame Madin to the Marquis and instructs him to send his reply to her letter to this woman's address: "[Madame Madin is] a worthy woman who was my friend and to whom you can address your reply. . . . Here is [her] address: *Madame Madin, Pavillon de Bourgogne, rue d'Anjou, Versailles*" (37). Grimm then goes on to give some "biographical" details about Suzanne's friend, informing us that she was the "wife of a former infantry officer, who really lived in Versailles" (38). And he explains why, from the conspirators' perspective, it had become necessary to enlist her help: "We needed an address to receive the [Marquis's] replies" (38). Madame Madin thus joins the ranks of the other conspirators and participates actively in the plot by forwarding all the letters postmarked Caen to the group in Paris.

To complicate matters even more, Madame Madin is both a character in the *Préface-annexe*—the one who supposedly forwards the letters—and, at a further fictional remove, one of the masks Diderot will eventually adopt in the correspondence or, in other words, the character Diderot who, as we shall see, at a later point writes under the guise of Madame Madin. It is important to understand at this juncture, however, that the Madame Madin to whom Grimm alludes has the same status as the other participants in the plot; like Grimm and Diderot, she is a fictional character who has been modeled on a real person. The word *real*, however, here refers only to the first level of the fiction, since it is impossible to determine not only whether the actual Madame Madin on whom Diderot modeled his character ever participated in the alleged plot but also whether the plot itself ever took place. (To distinguish between the "real" Madame Madin and Diderot writing as Madame Madin, then, the latter will henceforth be designated in my text within quotation marks.)

As it turns out, then, it is "Madame Madin" and not Suzanne who uses Suzanne's letter to communicate with the Marquis. It is not the content of Suzanne's letter that counts, but the way it functions as a pathway through which other people communicate about her.[5] The success of Suzanne's first letter lies, therefore, in the indirect pathways it initiates, which in turn add another level of complexity to the original circuit of communication. Her letter draws not just two more participants into the plot (the "real" Madame Madin and, later, Diderot writing under the guise of "Madame Madin") but potentially three, as the conspirators hoped that the Marquis's cousin would join forces with them: "This Governor [the Comte] . . . was just as weary of his cousin's absence as we were, and we hoped to include him in the ranks of the conspirators" (34). Furthermore, the detour that the letters themselves must take to Madame Madin's address in Versailles adds a third geographical location to the route they must travel, turning what had begun as a correspondence between Caen and Paris into a correspondence between Caen, Versailles, and Paris.

At this point, however, although the method of delivering the Marquis's letters to Suzanne has shifted from a direct to an indirect one, with "Madame Madin" functioning as messenger, the communicational circuit linking the two correspondents remains direct. When the Marquis answers Suzanne's first letter, he addresses his reply to "Mademoiselle [Simonin]" (39). Yet according to the model of communication that the *Préface-annexe* promotes, such an exchange should lead to the breakdown of the communicative process. And this is precisely what we now witness. In her second letter to the Marquis, Suzanne announces her illness and impending death, suggesting that the end of the epistolary exchange is imminent. But the correspondence does not end here, for it is at this very point that Diderot introduces the voice of "Madame Madin" (Diderot alias Madame Madin) as a third party in the circuit of communication. Thus by the time he answers Suzanne's second letter (the one in which she mentions her illness), the Marquis writes and addresses his letter not to Suzanne but to "Madame" (46). This is the beginning of the extensive correspondence between the Marquis and "Madame Madin" on *the subject of Suzanne.*

The inclusion of "Madame Madin" in the correspondence changes the process of communication itself from a direct to an indirect one via a third party and is, I would argue, the factor that allows it to continue: the correspondence had threatened to break down because Suzanne was dying, but once "Madame Madin" intervenes, she recuperates. And once again, the inclusion of another term in the circuit of communication adds another level of complexity to the system, for not only does Diderot now have to write in the place of two different characters (Suzanne and "Madame Madin"), but his doing so in turn necessitates the participation of yet another person, so that "Madame Madin's" letters will be written in a feminine handwriting different from the one found in Suzanne's letters: "for [Madame Madin's letters] we used the writing of another young woman" (38).

So far we have noted that the increasing complexity of the plot — note that here the word *plot* has to be understood in both senses, for the plot of this novelistic fragment is precisely furnished by the conspiratorial plot of Diderot and his cohorts — this plot is the result of the detours taken out of the direct circuit of communication between Suzanne and the Marquis, detours that lead out to the Comte de Croismare, the "real" Madame Madin, the fictional "Madame Madin," and the woman who transcribes the letters Diderot drafts for the latter. This process, however, takes an unexpected turn. Each time there is a detour *out* of the circuit of communication, the result is the *inclusion* of another participant in the plot and an expansion of the network of communicators.

One of the best confirmations that all pathways out of the circuit eventually lead back into it can be found near the end of the *Préface-annexe*, when "Madame Madin" confides to the Marquis a plan "she" has devised to procure a fixed income for Suzanne. The plan, of course, involves a third party, Madame de Tencin:

> I therefore thought that if we could somehow approach the Marquise de T***, who is said to be if not compassionate, at least very active . . . and if we could portray the sad situation of a young woman exposed to all the consequences of poverty . . . we might in this way extract a small income from the two brothers-in-law who took all of the family's possessions, and who have no intention of helping us. (53)

"Madame Madin" needs the Marquis's help, since "she" does not know anyone who could lobby on Suzanne's behalf with the Marquise de T***, and she hopes that the Marquis will. But, as previously noted in Grimm's explanation of "Madame Madin's" plan, it has been strategically designed by Diderot and the conspirators to force the Marquis to write to *Grimm*, the only friend of the Marquis's who would have access to Madame de T*** (50). Although we never find out whether the Marquis did write to Grimm, he does promise "Madame Madin" that he will: "I shall write at once to one of my friends, who can put you in touch with Madame de T***. His name is M. G***, First Secretary to Monsieur the Duke of Orléans" (61). Thus even the attempt to enlist the help of parties who have no apparent connection with the plot eventually leads right back into its very heart.

What is most remarkable about this progressive internalization, however, is that it goes one step further and changes the way the conspirators themselves perceive and experience the plot, gradually eliminating their intellectual and emotional distance from its events. The characters being included in the ever-expanding network of communicators internalize the affect, which then allows them to forget not to believe the fiction. This change is manifest in the way they allegedly begin to lose their ability to distinguish between fiction and reality.

At the beginning of the *Préface-annexe*, the protagonists are polarized into two camps. Diderot, Grimm, and the other conspirators view the events in the plot from an exterior, distanced perspective. They know that Suzanne does not exist; they are not taken in by Diderot's portrayal of her or the Marquis's emotional responses and can therefore laugh both at the letters Diderot composes with their collaboration and at the Marquis's answers: "We spent our suppers, amidst gales of laughter, reading letters that were supposed to make our good Marquis weep, and we also read with the same gales of laughter the sincere replies of our worthy and generous friend" (30). The Marquis, on the other hand, fully accepts the premises of the plot and therefore does not have any distance on the fiction; he is fully inside its framework and consequently is certain of the truth of something that for the others is a fiction. By the end of the *Préface-annexe*, however, the conspirators can no longer laugh when the decision is taken that Suzanne will be put to death: "The grief that her death caused us was hardly less acute than that of her honorable protector" (66). They are, so Grimm claims, just as much "victims" of the plot as the Marquis.

Nowhere is this change in perspective more dramatic, however, than in the case of Diderot. Indeed he is the first to change. According to Grimm, Diderot rapidly loses his "objective" perspective on the fiction of Suzanne: "While this mystification was kindling the imagination of our friend in Normandy, it was also kindling Diderot's" (30). Diderot is allegedly so fascinated by it that he undertakes to write the life story of Suzanne. One day, Grimm tells us, the actor d'Alainville finds the writing Diderot in tears and claiming, "I am deeply grieved by a story I am inventing" (31).

This scene produces a crucial reversal. Diderot is no longer in a position of mastery, able to keep his distance and maintain his objectivity on a fiction he himself has authored. His perspective now is analogous to the Marquis's; he can no longer "laugh" at the letters he drafts and at the Marquis's responses, but rather, like the Marquis, he is moved to tears by Suzanne's plight. The change in Diderot's position is thus underscored figuratively by the ironic presence of d'Alainville, who as an actor is generally the object of others' beholding. Here he becomes the spectator of Diderot's drama. Indeed there is a double irony here, for up to this point Diderot has been cast in the role of observer (of the Marquis's reactions, of his own participation in the plot and of that of the other conspirators), but now he becomes the object of someone else's scrutiny. This scene implicitly makes the point that Diderot, like the Marquis, is now a character in the same drama as Suzanne and the Marquis, whose role in the correspondence, as Grimm delights in telling us, "is not the least touching one in the novel" (65).

Grimm even claims that by the end of the plot Diderot "firmly believed that the Marquis and his own friends were playing a joke on him" (33). His suspicion that he is the one who is being fooled by the others reveals (or is supposed to reveal) the full extent of Diderot's involvement in a fiction of his own creation, to the point where he seems to have forgotten his own role as the instigator of the plot. Not only has fiction become as affective as reality for him, but reality seems to fade away altogether and be incorporated into the fiction, for now he perceives even the Marquis's letters as deliberate fakes.

Why does Diderot turn the tables and reverse the premises of the fiction, so that he now appears to be the victim of his own plot? His doing so suggests that, like other writers of epistolary fiction in the eighteenth century, he was trying to efface his own role as author. Unlike many of his contemporaries, however, Diderot does not hide behind the characters who allegedly write the letters by adopting the role of an ostensibly neutral editor or publisher. Diderot instead effaces himself as the author of his own text by deliberately putting himself at center stage, by creating the persona "Diderot" who interacts with the other "conspirators" and who, like them, loses all perspective on the story of Suzanne.[6] Moreover, Diderot goes on to undermine his own authority even further, as we shall see, by ceding the position of author to another participant in the plot.

It all begins with the Grimm persona, the narrator in the *Préface-annexe*. Grimm presents himself as the guarantor of the events of the plot, saying that "the letters signed Madin or Suzanne Simonin were fabricated by that child of Belial [Diderot], and that the letters from the nun's generous protector are authentic and were written in good faith" (33). Implicitly, by pointing to his ability to distinguish the truth ("the authentic letters") from the fiction ("the fabricated letters"), Grimm claims an external, objective view of the events. He maintains this position throughout the *Préface-annexe*, continually pointing to the ruses used by the conspirators behind the scenes. It is Grimm, after all, who informs us of Diderot's fear that "the Marquis and his own friends were playing a joke on him" (33). And the fact that it is Grimm who can still distinguish the "real" letters from the fabricated letters and who claims that Diderot no longer can, underscores the extent to which Diderot seems to have ceded his authority to Grimm.

In a text that is supposedly not a fiction but a historical account, the author's function is to be the guarantor of the reliability of the events recounted. In a fictional text, the author's authority is a function of the individual author's power to shape perceptions, and not of his or her ability to tell the truth. The ambiguous status of the *Préface-annexe* (Is it history? Is it fiction?) points up the difference between these two types of authority conventionally attributed to the author's voice. Diderot has displaced the position of historical authority onto the Grimm persona, a strategy that allows him seemingly to divest his voice in the text of this type of authority while still keeping some form of literary authority intact. But the situation is not so simple, for Diderot puts Grimm in this position only to pull the rug out from under him.

An incident at the end of the *Préface-annexe* illustrates clearly the full extent of Grimm's authorial takeover. Whereas at the beginning of his account of the plot Grimm had said that it was Diderot who made the decision to end Suzanne's life ("as soon as we realized that the fate of our unfortunate nun was beginning to interest her tender benefactor a little too much, M. Diderot decided to have her put to death" [30]), at the end of the *Préface-annexe* Grimm states merely: "This information left us no choice about the measures that had to be taken" (66). He no longer makes any reference to Diderot and erases him with the collective pronoun *us*.

But immediately after Grimm makes this assertion, the dramatic change takes place: "But as we had all taken on the feelings of Madame Madin for this interesting creature, the grief that her death caused us was hardly less acute than that of her honorable protector" (66). Grimm includes himself among those who have lost their "objectivity" concerning Suzanne. This point, however, is made more subtly than might be evident at first glance, for Grimm refers not to Diderot's feelings but to "the feelings of *Madame Madin*." He thereby reveals the extent to which he has lost his external, objective (historical) viewpoint and is now *inside* the fiction, for he no longer sees Diderot writing the letters signed "Madame Madin," as he had in the beginning ("the letters signed Madin . . . were fabricated by that child of Belial" [33]). Instead he sees only Madame Madin, grieving over the problems of Suzanne.

Grimm's capitulation undermines the very notion of authority and with it the position of objective exteriority that we saw Diderot cede to him. Neither Diderot—the author and instigator of the plot—nor Grimm—the narrator, eyewitness, and participant in the plot—can maintain it. This is precisely the point that the *Préface-annexe* makes relentlessly: even those who *know* that the events of the plot are nothing more than a fictional creation, who have themselves participated in inventing and activating its machinery, cannot maintain their distance from it.

But there are other ways in which Grimm's position and perspective are weakened. Among them are the hints given in the *Préface-annexe* that perhaps Grimm does not have the definitive knowledge he claims to possess. Grimm, for instance, asserts that "the Marquis never suspected for an instant a perfidy that we had on our consciences for a long time" (29–30), an assertion that he reinforces with the story of the night, many years after the plot had ended, when the Marquis met the "real" Madame Madin: "It was a real *coup de théâtre*: Monsieur de Croismare had been intending to make a thousand inquiries about the unfortunate young woman who had so greatly interested him, and about whose existence Madame Madin knew nothing at all" (38–39). Yet Grimm's judgment that the Marquis was the unwitting victim of the plot is put into question by one of the Marquis's letters, in which he appears to be suspicious of "Madame Madin's" plan to establish an income for Suzanne, thereby throwing doubt upon Grimm's portrayal of the Marquis as someone who is unambiguously naive.[7]

Furthermore, as the plot unfolds, a bizarre incident, involving the wax seal placed by the Marquis on one of the letters he had sent to Suzanne, casts serious doubts on Grimm's credibility (and, for that matter, on the credibility of all the participants in the plot). In the letter in question, the Marquis de Croismare urges Suzanne to save his seal so that she can use it later to identify herself upon her arrival in Caen. In her reply to the Marquis, Suzanne assures him that she will follow his instructions carefully. She then describes the seal she has found on his letter in the following terms: "There is a holy angel stamped on it; it is you, it is my guardian angel" (41). This description of the image on the Marquis's seal, however, is at odds with Grimm's, as we learn in the narrative passage that precedes the text of Suzanne's letter. Where the young woman sees a guardian angel, Grimm sees a cupid: "The seal represented a cupid holding a torch in one hand and two hearts in the other, with a motto that we were unable to read, because the seal had been damaged when the letter was opened" (40).

The discrepancy between Grimm's description of the Marquis's seal and Suzanne's serves at a primary level, of course, to put into focus the difference between his perspective and hers. Whereas Grimm and the other conspirators can interpret the potentially erotic connotations of the image on the seal, Suzanne, to remain consistent with her portrayal as an innocent young nun, must be unable to read its iconography in other than religious terms.

But there is more at stake in Suzanne's allusion to the Marquis's seal. As it happens, the letter in which she mentions the "guardian angel" was drafted not by Diderot, who was unable to attend one of the conspirators' meetings, but by Grimm and the others. However, when Diderot reads the letter that his cohorts had composed in his absence, he angrily insists that the words they have put in Suzanne's mouth will give away the entire plot: "[Suzanne's reply] was not to [Diderot's] liking; he maintained that it would expose our treachery" (41). Grimm, on the other hand, insists that Diderot is wrong: "[Diderot] was mistaken, and he was wrong, I think, to dislike [the reply we had drafted on Suzanne's behalf]" (41). Although we are never informed of Diderot's specific objections to the letter sent by Grimm and his partners in crime, there is some evidence that Suzanne's "misinterpretation" of the image that the conspirators had seen on the Marquis's seal is indeed the bone of contention in Grimm's dispute with Diderot.[8]

In "her" next letter to the Marquis, "Madame Madin" tells him pointedly that "[Suzanne] is keeping the seal from your letter. . . . I didn't dare tell her that it wasn't yours; I had broken it when I opened your letter and replaced it with mine. Given the sorry state she's in, I couldn't risk giving her your letter without reading it first" (43–44). If "Madame Madin" (Diderot) feels compelled to tell the Marquis that "she" has substituted "her" own seal for his (presumably as a way of explaining Suzanne's allusion to the "guardian angel"), this can only mean that the seal the conspirators had seen was *different* from the one the Marquis had put on his letter and that *Diderot* is the only one who is aware of this. (We know from Grimm's earlier statements that he and the other conspirators are convinced that the cupid seal is the Marquis's own). It would then follow that Diderot must have replaced the seal without telling the others before they saw the Marquis's letter, and that this is the reason why he fears Suzanne's reference to the "guardian angel" in the letter drafted by Grimm will give away the plot. Whereas the argument I have just sketched out is perfectly logical, there is no textual evidence to substantiate that this event ever took place.

Another conclusion is equally plausible. The Marquis may have used the cupid seal on his letter after all, and if so this would mean that the conspirators had been deliberately hiding its existence from Diderot. As a result, it could be Diderot who gives himself away when he has "Madame Madin" tell the Marquis that "she" replaced his seal with "hers."

Which of the two possibilities is given to the reader as the true one? Who knows more, Grimm and the other conspirators or Diderot? Who is right, Diderot or Grimm and the other conspirators? It is impossible to give a definitive answer to these questions. What this incident illustrates so powerfully is that none of the conspirator characters has a totalizing position from which he or she can view all of the components of the plot and therefore know the full truth of what is taking place. As a result, no one's version of what is "happening" in the plot is entirely reliable — not even Grimm's.

Finally, the incident of the Marquis's seal directs our attention to the one missing element in the preceding analysis. If neither Diderot nor Grimm and the other conspirators can maintain the external position and perspective (needless to say, the Marquis cannot), then who does? Presumably, as in other epistolary novels, the reader. But this is an assumption that the *Préface-annexe* also undermines, a point that becomes clear if we reread Grimm's role in terms of the function he fulfills for the reader.[9]

The Grimm character as witness creates the illusion that the reader is privy to all the machinations of the conspirators and therefore sees everything that happens "behind the scenes." He alludes frequently to his role in granting the reader the perspective of a privileged eyewitness, stating for instance, "I shall place before your eyes [the correspondence] between M. Diderot, or the would-be nun, and the loyal and charming Marquis de Croismare" (29). Grimm, furthermore, instructs the reader on how he should read: "Please remember that the letters signed Madin, or Suzanne Simonin, were fabricated by [Diderot], and that the letters of the nun's generous protector are authentic" (33).* And he constantly demystifies the ruses

---

*Diderot specifically addresses both the *Préface-annexe* and the rest of *La Religieuse* to male readers. In the *Préface-annexe*, Diderot identifies these readers as the "men of letters" to whom he poses a question at the end of the text. The narrative of *La Religieuse* is not only ostensibly addressed to the Marquis de Croismare, but in it Diderot also explicitly uses the convention of the female seductive voice as the third term that allows one man to communicate with an-the conspirators use on the Marquis. Thanks to Grimm, for example, when "Madame Madin" tells the Marquis that he can "take everything I shall tell you [about Suzanne] to the letter" (44), the irony in her statement does not escape the reader, who knows it is impossible to take anything "Madame Madin" says literally, because "she" is Diderot and Diderot is inventing the story of Suzanne as the correspondence progresses.

The point of having Grimm fulfill this omniscient role is that with each demystificatory statement he conveys to the reader the confidence that he has the key, that he really knows what is taking place. But this is only an illusion of mastery, since the claims to omniscience of the figure who makes the distinctions between fact and fiction for the reader are gradually demystified in the course of the *Préface-annexe*.

Hence the reader's access to the events of the "plot" — through Grimm — positions him at Grimm's own vantage point, which ends up being analogous and not superior to that of the "conspirators."[10] By making the reader think he has a privileged point of view, but by constructing the text in such a way that the reader is in fact in the same position as the con-

---

other. (It can be argued, as Chapter 5 will show, that Diderot also uses this convention in the *Rêve de d'Alembert* and therefore most likely is assuming a male reader for this text as well.) Furthermore, in the introduction to the *Essai sur les règnes de Claude et de Néron*, Diderot identifies his reader as a "man age sixty-five or sixty-six," a "man of genius," or "an upstanding man." This is not to say that there was no female readership for Diderot's texts or even that Diderot himself might not in some instances have had a female reader in mind. However, in order to take into account Diderot's explicit address to male readers, and to maintain stylistic unity throughout my text, I shall use the masculine pronoun when referring to the reader in the present work.

For perceptive discussion of Diderot's use of the convention of the female seductive voice in *La Religieuse*, see Jay Caplan, *Framed Narratives: Diderot's Genealogy of the Beholder* (Minneapolis: University of Minnesota Press, 1985). For an interesting perspective on the operation of gender in Diderot's writings, see Elisabeth de Fontenay, *Diderot ou le matérialisme enchanté* (Paris: Grasset, 1981); and Rita Goldberg, *Sex and Enlightenment: Women in Richardson and Diderot* (New York: Cambridge University Press, 1984).

spirators vis-à-vis these facts, the *Préface-annexe* destabilizes the reader's position, a process whose ultimate goal is to draw the reader in, to make him an active participant in the fiction. One example is provided in the "letter that was never sent," which interrupts the exchange of letters between the principal correspondents. This is the letter that Diderot proposes as a substitute for the one that Grimm and the others drafted and sent in his absence and which Diderot believes will give away the plot. The text of Diderot's letter is included in the *Préface-annexe*, as Grimm says, "to satisfy him" (42).

This letter was not sent because it was not meant for the Marquis. Yet it is included in the text of the *Préface-annexe* as a piece of information that is available only to the conspirators. It has been added here for the reader, who in this way becomes a party to the conspiracy— "one of them."[11]

This event in the *Préface-annexe* seems to be another instance of a process analyzed earlier, that of the detours out of the circuit of communication whose end result is the inclusion of another communicator within it. The letter that is not sent but is nevertheless reproduced is such a detour, designed ultimately to engage the reader in the fiction. This moment in the text makes the reader aware that all the strategies put into play in the *Préface-annexe* are aimed ultimately at him. The reader's relationship to the *Préface-annexe* is mirrored in the conspirators' relationship to the correspondence. What is specifically at stake in these strategies is the undermining of the reader's position of distanced exteriority. The *Préface-annexe*, as we have seen, gradually abolishes within its textual economy the position of distanced exteriority held at various times by the characters in order to act out the same process with the reader and make it impossible for him to maintain that position.

This hypothesis has disturbing implications for any critic who undertakes an interpretation of this text. If indeed the

Préface-annexe is successful in accomplishing its goal, then it makes untenable the critic's own presumably distanced position. But there is no way of proving that the *Préface-annexe* does what I claim it does, for if this is the case, I myself would inevitably have been caught in its net at some point, and therefore my view of this text would already have been influenced by its destabilizing strategies. As such, any claim on my part to understand the strategies this text puts into play would automatically be questionable, because my own position would be just as unstable as that of any other critic. The only substantiation of my claim about the untenability of the critic's position vis-à-vis the *Préface-annexe* that I can offer is indirect, an analysis of the two most distinguished critical readings of the *Préface-annexe*: Georges May's and Herbert Dieckmann's.

Georges May's first reading of the *Préface-annexe* — found in his book *Diderot et "La Religieuse"* — provides an exemplary case. When May discusses the *Préface-annexe* in this work, he is always fully inside the premises of the fiction; he has no position outside, because for him the *Préface-annexe* recounts the historical events that led to the writing of the novel *La Religieuse*. He even goes so far as to use the term *document* when referring to the *Préface-annexe* and the phrase *pieces of information* when referring to the events it recounts.[12] His critical operation, therefore, consists of finding historical records to prove that the events portrayed in the *Préface-annexe* really took place: he establishes the biographical facts of the Marquis de Croismare's life (which corroborate Grimm's description of him in the *Préface-annexe*) and the circumstances of the trial of the real nun, Marguerite Delamarre, who in his view was Diderot's model for Suzanne Simonin.

Because May sees the *Préface-annexe* as fact and not fiction, he reads this text literally. Thus, for example, he retells the anecdote of d'Alainville that appears in the *Préface-annexe* as if it were an event that had actually occurred.

By dint of holding the would-be nun's pen along with his friends, Diderot got so carried away that he himself ended up believing in the existence of the poor girl, in her sufferings and her pitiful condition. . . . The *Préface-annexe* recounts a telling anecdote in this regard. While the philosopher was busy composing the memoirs of the nun, his friend d'Alainville came to visit him and found him overwhelmed by sorrow, his face streaming with tears. "What is wrong?" d'Alainville asked him; "what a state you're in." "What is wrong," Diderot answered, "is that I am deeply grieved by a story I am inventing." Let us therefore forgive Diderot, given the beauty of this anecdote and the goodness of his heart, for having taken part in such a bad practical joke.[13]

May's historical approach prevents him from taking a critical distance on the events recounted in the *Préface-annexe*.

Herbert Dieckmann's "The *Préface-annexe* of *La Religieuse*" threw new light on the problem of the historical actuality of the events recounted in this text. Dieckmann discovered a manuscript of the *Préface-annexe* in the Fonds Vandeul with corrections and additions written in Diderot's own hand. These corrections revealed that Diderot had revised the 1760 manuscript of the *Préface-annexe* between 1780 and 1781 and, more important, that he meant the *Préface-annexe* to be an integral part of the fiction of *La Religieuse*: "The changes [Diderot] made considerably modify the style of the preface and his additions completely alter its character. The *Préface-annexe* can no longer be considered as a document which gives the biographical and historical background of *La Religieuse*, the 'true story' behind the 'fiction' of the novel . . . it is as much invention and fable as the novel itself."[14]

As a result of his findings, Dieckmann goes to the opposite extreme from May and argues in favor of the fictionality of the *Préface-annexe*. And in Dieckmann's assertion that everything recounted in the *Préface-annexe* is a fiction, he seems able at first to maintain a critical distance on its premises. But there is more in Dieckmann's article. He points out that the anecdote of d'Alainville, which May had read as proof positive that Diderot indeed had become so involved in the story of Suzanne that he began to think she was a real person, is one of the additions that Diderot made in 1780–81 to the 1760 manuscript of the *Préface-annexe*.[15] After making this observation, however, Dieckmann seems curiously unable to make up his own mind. His interpretation of the d'Alainville anecdote from this point on oscillates between the poles of fiction and reality. At times he sees it as fiction, at times he seems to take it at face value.

Let us consider, for example, Dieckmann's comment on the traditional reading of the anecdote: "The story has often been used by biographers to illustrate and emphasize Diderot's sensitivity and sentimentality." One would expect Dieckmann's next statement to be a refutation of that interpretation, but instead he seems to backtrack and to speculate that d'Alainville's visit may have taken place: "This interpretation is not altogether wrong, nor is the story an invention simply because Diderot himself told it. D'Alainville probably called on Diderot, found him in tears, and received the surprising answer."[16] However, Jacques Chouillet warns in a recent article on the *Préface-annexe*: "We must take with a grain of salt the anecdotes (which [Diderot] himself obligingly recounts) that show [him] in the process of weeping over a story he has just composed. . . . It is not at all certain that he was caught in the trap of his own sentimentality to the extent that he claims."[17] Dieckmann's intuition had already suggested to him that a literal interpretation of this anecdote is too simple; hence the final step in his discussion is an attempt to identify the irony in it: "But we must now add that Diderot . . . the man of judgment, could tell a good story about Diderot 'homme sensible.' One may go further and say that an author who, after many years, inserted such an anecdote into an account which quite evidently was written by someone else, and who, by so doing, deliberately misled the reader, must have had a reason for it."[18] Dieckmann thus seems to end his discussion of the d'Alainville anecdote from a position of critical distance and apparently tends to interpret it as a fictional device.

But this is not the last time the d'Alainville anecdote appears in Dieckmann's article. Toward the end of it, Dieckmann comments on Grimm's allegation that by the end of the plot all the conspirators had been taken in.

> There is certainly a touch of irony in this account, but only a touch; the Mme Madin of the letters, one must recall, was also a fictitious character. Decidedly it was no longer possible to tell reality from fiction. Even Diderot himself, who was the inventor of the entire story, was under the illusion. The anecdote about d'Alainville's visit shows it in an amusing way: "I am deeply grieved by a story I am inventing." Where did fiction begin and reality end?[19]

Dieckmann has fallen into the trap. Although he asserts repeatedly that the *Préface-annexe* is a fiction, and therefore presumably can retain his distance, he ends up taking the same stance as Georges May, accepting the claim that the story of Suzanne was so compelling that in fact it ensnared not only the Marquis, Grimm, and the other conspirators but even Diderot, its own creator.

Therefore, like the "plot" in the *Préface-annexe*, Dieckmann's article takes "an altogether different turn" (29). The way it begins and the way it ends are totally different and reveal that Dieckmann, although aware of the tricks in the *Préface-annexe*, ends up falling for them anyway. It is for this very reason that Dieckmann's reading is so interesting, for his ability to see the fictionality of the account does not prevent his developing a blindness to it. This is exactly what we saw happening consistently to all the conspirators. Dieckmann may thus have achieved what Diderot might consider a perfect reading of the *Préface*: his awareness of its tricks does not preclude their *effectiveness*. The *Préface-annexe* works.

We can now go back and try to read the d'Alainville anecdote in a different light. To do this it is necessary to displace the focus of the discussion away from the issue debated in the traditional criticism of the *Préface-annexe*, the issue of whether Diderot, Grimm, and the Marquis all "really" fell for the fiction of Suzanne. This is not the important question; rather, what is important here is that Diderot represents himself, Grimm, and the Marquis as having fallen for it. Now, of course, the question is why? We can ask, for instance, what it means for an author to portray himself as a character in a fiction, one who, moreover, is in a position of nonmastery vis-à-vis a fable of his own creation. How does such a move affect the classical notion of authorship?

A well-known concrete illustration of this dismantling of authority is the *Encyclopédie*, whose status remains that of an "authorless" text, insofar as the multiplicity of authors of its numerous articles prevents any one individual from being defined as *the* single author. To ensure that no one will ever hold such a position, furthermore, the *Encyclopédie* uses a system of cross-references, whose purpose is actively to encourage the production and circulation of meaning.

In his essay "What Is an Author?" Michel Foucault maintains that fiction is a subversive discourse, one whose capacity to generate a multiplicity of meanings threatens social order, since it defies any neat systems of classification. To counteract this situation, to bring fiction's "proliferation of meanings" under control, traditional criticism defines the author as "the genial creator of a work in which he deposits, with infinite wealth and generosity, an inexhaustible world of significations," thus displacing the problem of the multiplicity of meanings in fiction away from the domain of the text onto the single figure of the author. Foucault uses this displacement from text to author to argue precisely the contrary, saying that the author "is a certain functional principle by which, in our culture, one limits, excludes, and chooses; in short, by which one impedes the free circulation, the free manipulation, the free composition, decomposition, and recomposition of fiction."[20] Foucault focuses specifically on the social use of the "author-function," analyzing the process whereby it can be imposed from the outside as a means of suppressing the subversive power of fiction. Diderot, for his part, already foreseeing this possibility, attempts to prevent his reader from imposing the author-function by explicitly subverting it from within.

I would argue that to assume and ensure his fiction's full potential, Diderot attempts to free it from the constraints of authorial power by fictionalizing himself in the *Préface-annexe* and by systematically undermining the position of anyone who attempts to reinstate the author-function. His lifting of the constraints of the author-function in turn has implications for the reader, who will thereby gain access to the "free circulation" of fiction. For Diderot, however, this does not mean that the power and control he has wrested from the author-function is transferred to the reader. The kind of relationship he seeks to construct between author and reader is one in which neither is in a position of mastery with respect to the other; Diderot seeks to destabilize the position of both the reader and the author. This radicalization of the relationship between the "reader-function" and the author is one of the *Préface-annexe*'s major narrative innovations.

Nevertheless it is obvious that in this relationship the author still has a potential advantage, since he can act on the reader through his text, whereas the reader is powerless to act either on the author or on the text. Despite Diderot's efforts to undermine his own authorial power, we can speculate that he was aware of the reader's greater vulnerability to the seduction operated by fictional texts. That indeed Diderot was acutely aware of fiction's potential for seduction is evidenced by the "Eloge de Richardson," in which he describes his amazement at the affective response Richardson's novels could generate.[21] As if to protect his readers from the overwhelming power of fiction, therefore, Diderot makes its strategically conceived mechanisms obvious to them. This is one of the roles the *Préface-annexe* fulfills, providing a look "behind the scenes" at the machinery of the fiction. Thus, having "demystified" the author-function, Diderot ends the *Préface-annexe* with the "Question to Men of Letters."

> M. Diderot, after having spent whole mornings composing letters that were well crafted, well thought out, thoroughly romanesque, and laden with pathos, would then spend whole days spoiling those same letters by suppressing, on the advice of his wife and his partners in crime, everything in them that was striking or seemed exaggerated, everything that was not in keeping with the utmost simplicity and verisimilitude; so that if someone had picked up the first group of letters on the street, he would have said: This is beautiful, very beautiful. . . . And if someone had picked up the second group, he would have said: This is very true to life. . . . Which letters were better? Those that might have won admiration? Or those that were certain to produce the illusion?   (67–68)

In this passage, Diderot provides a final reminder for the reader that the *Préface-annexe* is not a "natural" transcription of a series of historical events, but rather a carefully constructed and reworked artifice, based on specific esthetic criteria. Diderot, in other words, purposely shows the reader at every turn that no artifice of the fiction is being hidden but that, on the contrary, all artifices are being continually unveiled. But we should not conclude from this, as many early critics of *La Religieuse* did, that

Diderot's attempts to warn his reader about the seductive strategies of fiction destroy the illusion that the text should be attempting to create. As we saw in the case of Dieckmann's reading of the *Préface-annexe*, an awareness of this text's stratagems does not impair their effectiveness. This point raises a serious critical question for which at this point I can only suggest an answer.

By reminding the reader relentlessly of the stratagems in his fiction, Diderot makes the reader aware that he is the object of a carefully planned and strategically conceived seduction. But such an awareness amounts to seducing him in a noncoercive way, for the implicit assumption here is that the pleasure of giving in to a *staged* seduction—that the reader can identify as such—is greater than the pleasure the reader would derive from being unwillingly manipulated by a *surreptitious* seduction. Diderot's unveiling of the mechanisms of his fiction is, therefore, a double-edged strategy that ends up working doubly in his favor, for he not only manages to warn the reader about his own susceptibility to fiction but, by so doing, encourages him to participate willingly in his own downfall.

This hypothesis is corroborated by the "Eloge de Richardson," which tells of Richardson's ability to seduce the reader by drawing him into the fiction, thus abolishing his distanced objectivity. According to Diderot, two factors—action and detail—fulfill this function in Richardson's novels.

First, action encourages the reader's active participation and disrupts the dichotomy between outside and inside: "He who acts is the one who draws our attention, we put ourselves in his place or at his side. . . . O Richardson! in spite of ourselves, we take a role in your works."[22] The movement implicit in the representation of action affects the reader, sweeping him up in its dynamic and thereby producing the spatial illusion that he has been incorporated into the universe of the fiction.

Second, Diderot attributes to Richardson's strategic use of

details the blurring for the reader of the distinction between fiction and reality.

> Be aware that the illusion depends on this multitude of minor details . . . it is these truths of detail that prepare the soul for the strong impressions produced by great events. Once your impatience has been suspended by those momentary delays that were serving as dams for it, with what recklessness won't it pour forth at the moment when it pleases the poet to break down those dams. At that point, whether overcome by grief or transported by joy, you will no longer have the strength to hold back the tears that have been on the verge of flowing nor to say to yourself: *But perhaps that isn't true.* This thought will have been distanced from your mind little by little.[23]

What is at stake in Diderot's analysis of Richardson's use of details is time. In Diderot's view, Richardson's long, drawn-out descriptions, which result from the emphasis he places on details, are dilatory tactics whose strategic efficacy can be attributed to the destabilizing effect they have on the reader. The play of temporality they activate — the constant postponement of the progression of the narrative — produces a change in the reader's perception; it draws the reader into the fiction, abolishing the distance that would otherwise allow him to discriminate between what is outside (reality) and inside (fiction). The reader is thus placed firmly *inside*, in that region where fiction *becomes* reality for him.

All the preceding observations allow us to reconsider traditional notions of Diderot's "realism." Critics such as Georges May, Herbert Dieckmann, and Vivienne Mylne have defined that realism as being the product of the mimetic relationship that Diderot's texts maintain with "reality." Dieckmann, for example, asserts that "Diderot . . . clung stubbornly to the dogma that realism can only be achieved by direct imitation of actual events and veristic description of actual persons."[24] I propose instead that Diderot's realism is a function of the relationship that his fictional texts construct and maintain with the reader. For Diderot the illusion of reality (which seems to be what Dieckmann means by "realism") is created when the text succeeds in incorporating the reader as an integral term of the fiction. It is as a consequence of the reader's destabilization that the experience of fiction will be activated, that the illusion of reality will be produced.

In the "Eloge de Richardson," Diderot merely analyzes the narrative strategies Richardson employs in his novels — and especially those he uses to destabilize the reader's position. In the *Préface-annexe*, however, we see Diderot working out his *own* strategies for accomplishing the same goal. I would therefore read the *Préface-annexe* — rather than the "Eloge de Richardson" — as the text in which Diderot most fully articulates his theory of fiction. But if I am right in claiming that the *Préface-annexe* should be viewed as a more comprehensive theoretical text than the "Eloge," then we must also conclude that for Diderot a theory of fiction is best elaborated within fiction itself, for the *Préface-annexe* contains both a theory (as it proposes a particular set of destabilizing strategies) and a practice (as the very formulation of these strategies is done within the framework of a text that already puts them to use).

As the "Question to Men of Letters" had already shown, the issue of the difference between beauty and verisimilitude is left in suspension. By shifting the focus to structures and practices of communication, Diderot suggests that an answer cannot be given in abstract terms. Fiction is accessible not through abstractions but through the experience that the text activates and the reader undergoes.

The inseparability of theory and practice in the *Préface-annexe* may also account for the peculiar difficulties this text poses for critics. In general, critics have always been affected by this text's operation, a fact that in turn puts into question any critic's claim to understanding. The only option, then, is for the critic to acknowledge that he or she is always already subject to the destabilizing action of the *Préface-annexe* and that, as a consequence, any pretension to critical certainty is untenable. The *Préface-annexe* provides Diderot's reader with a practical theory of indirect or ternary communication, which Diderot then elaborates and puts to the test in the body of *La Religieuse*.

CHAPTER THREE

MUSICAL CONVERSATIONS

NARRATIVE MODELS AND COMMUNICATION IN "LA RELIGIEUSE"

This conversation, in which I include you as a third.
— Diderot, *Lettres à Sophie Volland*

"Everything I say comes out skewed" (*"Je dis tout de travers"*).[1] Suzanne Simonin formulates her inadaptation to convent life in these terms. What this statement reveals, however, is not so much her inability to adapt to the circumstances in which she finds herself, but rather her skill at turning impossible situations to her advantage. As Suzanne discovers early in life, conventional modes of communication do not work for her. For this reason, far from being the *wrong* way of saying things, speaking "de travers" — which should be understood to mean obliquely, indirectly — is the only communicative strategy available to her, a strategy that she develops in the course of her years in various convents. To understand why Suzanne must rely on such a strategy to make herself understood, however, it is necessary to take into account her worldly situation.

Because of her illegitimate birth, Suzanne Simonin's very existence constitutes a disruption in the social order and in the stability of the family. By extension, she creates disruptions wherever she goes. In the context of her family, for instance, Suzanne becomes an obstacle to the marriage of one of her two sisters when, because of her superior beauty and talents, she attracts the attention of her sister's suitor. And once both sisters are married, Suzanne becomes a potential source of "disorder" (41; *110*) and "dissension" (38; *106*) in their domestic lives, as her own mother cruelly points out. In her mother's life, furthermore, Suzanne is a "poison" (40; *109*) and, according to one of the family's servants, the only source of disharmony in her parents' marriage.

Rejected by her mother and stepfather as a result of the disturbances that her presence in the family continually provokes, Suzanne's problems are compounded by her parents' refusal to give her a dowry, thus depriving her of the possibility of integration into society through marriage. Instead her parents exile her to a convent. But, as a nun without vocation, radically different from her fellow nuns by virtue of her intransigent rejection of the role she has been assigned, Suzanne cannot integrate herself into the religious community either. There too she can only create disruptions. In one convent, Suzanne creates a scandal by publicly refusing to take vows; in another her resistance to monastic life disrupts the cohesion of the religious community, to the point where she is accused of being "Satan" (85; *163*). Suzanne's perturbatory powers are such that she even has a harmful effect on Soeur Ursule, her only friend in the convent; Suzanne quite literally kills her—Soeur Ursule dies after catching an illness from Suzanne.

Her alienation from the contexts in which she must exist, however, manifests itself most clearly in her inability to make herself understood. Experience teaches her that normal channels of communication are closed to her. Direct dialogue again and again proves ineffective. Throughout the novel, Suzanne's numerous entreaties to her parents are resounding failures. To cite one instance, Suzanne's attempts to dissuade her parents from forcing her to take preliminary vows are in vain: "I saw my father and mother, I spared no effort to touch their hearts, but found them inflexible" (25; *89*). At a later point, a pathetic appeal for her mother's sympathy and understanding has no effect: "I . . . seized one of her hands and . . . kissed it, saying: 'You are still my mother, I am still your child.' She answered (pushing me even more roughly and snatching her hand away from mine): 'Get up, wretched girl, get up' "(34; *102*). In the second convent, a conversation in which Suzanne tries to convince the superior to help her escape yields only negative results. The superior not only refuses to help her, but in addition forces her to undergo a series of brutal punishments (78–83; *155–61*).

Letters seem to be just as ineffective as dialogue. Those she sends to her family during her stay in the first convent, in which she expresses her distaste for convent life and asks for permission to leave, only succeed in prolonging her captivity. And when, at a later point, Suzanne writes to her sisters begging them not to oppose her initiative to have her vows annulled, she receives the reply: "We must thwart this dangerous endeavor with all our might" (74; *151*).

Letters and dialogue having failed her, Suzanne—in a desperate attempt to convey to her family her wish to leave the convent—decides to stage a theatrical performance of sorts during her vow-taking ceremony. By now realizing the futility of addressing her appeal exclusively to her parents, she selects and invites a wider "audience" of family members and friends whose sympathy and assistance she hopes to enlist. On the day of the ceremony, she dons her "costume" for the scene: "They came to adorn me; this day is a day for dressing up" (32; *99*). Everything seems to go smoothly during the ceremony until the priest asks whether she accepts the vows of poverty, chastity, and obedience. Contrary to everyone's expectations, Suzanne answers that she does not. Furthermore, to ensure that there will be no doubt about her intention, she turns to face the audience and declares: "Gentlemen, and you especially, my own father and mother, I call you all to witness" (33; *101*). Immediately another nun lets the curtain of the altar grill fall, signaling the end of Suzanne's "performance." Despite her efforts and planning, then, Suzanne's audacious action ends in disaster. Although the public scandal she creates forces her parents to take her out of the convent for a while, in the long run it only reinforces their determination to send her back again, as they eventually do. Suzanne's action so angers the other nuns that immediately following the ceremony they lock her up in a cell.

Suzanne thus meets with failure at every turn in her attempts to communicate her repugnance for religious life and her desperate need for freedom. She creates disruptions not just in the social order but in all circuits of direct communication, rendering them dysfunctional. For this reason, Suzanne's only hope is to find a strategy for communication that will make disruption work in her favor. This is precisely what Madame de Moni, the first superior of the convent at Longchamp, provides her. In sharp contrast to Suzanne's ineffective appeals, Madame de Moni's exchanges with the nuns who seek her counsel are prototypes of effective communication. When Suzanne, for example, turns to her for consolation, Madame de Moni at first reasons with her and then offers reassuring words: "My good Mother Superior . . . strengthened my spirit, reasoned powerfully with me and always ended by saying 'And don't other walks in life have their thorns also?' " (47; *118*) But Madame de Moni understands that dialogue will never bring about her ends. Instead she prays and exhorts her interlocutor to pray with her: "Come along, my child, let us kneel down and pray" (47; *118*). Indeed it is only when she is engaged in prayer that Madame de Moni can obtain the result she seeks: "She would then prostrate herself and pray aloud. . . . Her thoughts, her expressions, her images, penetrated deep into your heart. At first you listened, then little by little you were swept along, you became one with her, your soul thrilled and you shared her ecstasy" (47; *118–19*). Madame de Moni succeeds in comforting her interlocutors not by addressing them directly but by addressing herself to God.

If we look at the instances cited previously of Suzanne's unsuccessful attempts to communicate, we can see that they all have one element in common: they are direct exchanges. When she engages in a dialogue, when she writes letters, and even when she stages a performance, Suzanne addresses her interlocutors directly. And, as the comparison with Madame de Moni's procedure suggests, this is precisely what Suzanne does wrong. This is the textual realization of the ternary model of communication elaborated in the *Préface-annexe*. In the scenes with Madame de Moni, God, addressed through prayer, in much the same way as Suzanne's first letter to the Marquis de Croismare, acts as the third term that transforms the act of communication from a direct to an indirect one. Furthermore, interruption is an integral part of the communicative process according to the terms of this model. In the case of Madame de Moni, her prayers interrupt the conversation with Suzanne (she must turn away from Suzanne to address God), but this interruption ultimately facilitates the transmission of her message (Suzanne finds solace only *through* Madame de Moni's prayers). Therefore, in this scene, communication is defined as a process in which disruptions in the circuit do not impede the exchange of information but instead take on a positive function, generating a more complex and more effective form of communication.

Suzanne immediately applies Madame de Moni's method and discovers that it works: "I interrupted or even anticipated her or spoke along with her" (71; *148*). These disruptions, however, no longer have adverse effects. Instead they produce moments of privileged communication, moments when the communion between the two praying interlocutors is so perfect that they appear to be of one mind: "When she prayed aloud, I would sometimes begin to speak, follow the thread of her thoughts and find, as if by inspiration, part of what she would have said herself" (71; *148*). Though Suzanne's way of interacting with Madame de Moni differs from that of the other nuns, who instead of interrupting sit and listen quietly to the superior's prayers (71; *148*), Suzanne's unorthodox procedure is ultimately more effective. Whereas normally her interlocutors are the only ones to benefit from exchanges with Madame de Moni, the exchanges with Suzanne have a different effect. They leave their mark not just on Suzanne, but also on Madame de Moni herself: "If one could discern in the other nuns that they had conversed with her, one could discern in her that she had conversed with me" (72; *148*). In other words, by turning what would otherwise be a one-way exchange into a two-way exchange, Suzanne's interruptions produce a richer form of communication.

They do so also in another instance, again involving Madame de Moni. Vanquishing Suzanne's resistance to monastic life becomes a life or death struggle for the superior. As the time for Suzanne's final vows approaches, she exerts all her powers to reconcile Suzanne to her impending fate. But Madame de Moni's efforts end in failure, a failure that has dire consequences for her. First, she loses her talent for consolation; as Suzanne informs us, "Her gift abandoned her; she herself admitted it to me" (48; *119*). Then she loses her capacity to communicate with God: "'Ah, my dear child,' she said, 'what a cruel effect you have had on me! It is over and done with, I can feel that the Holy Spirit has withdrawn'" (48; *120*). In the end, Suzanne's invincible resistance seems to precipitate Madame de Moni's death. Almost immediately after she realizes that she has failed, the superior becomes ill and announces her impending death. In spite of this desperate situation, however, all is not lost. While she awaits her death, the superior writes a book of meditations: "She left behind fifteen meditations which seem to me of the greatest beauty. . . . They are entitled *The Last Moments of Soeur de Moni*" (53; 125). Madame de Moni's spiritual outpourings, though permanently disrupted in their spoken version, nevertheless are redeemed in their written version. This document, in turn, redeems her death by immortalizing her. And not the least of the book's advantages is that it can reach a wider audience because it can be circulated even among those outside the convent. As Suzanne is quick to point out: "I have a copy of [her meditations]. If one day you were curious to see the thoughts that our last moments evoke, I could send them to you" (53; 125). Paradoxically, then, the harm Suzanne at first does to Madame de Moni ultimately yields positive results by provoking the superior to turn her talents to writing and thereby produce the only possible permanent testament to her unusual gifts.

Madame de Moni plays a key role in Suzanne's life; her experiences with the superior teach her the one strategy that can turn her disadvantages into advantages, the strategy that allows her to begin communicating with others. But other incidents in Suzanne's life also reinforce the superior's lessons. After Madame de Moni's death, a tableau of Suzanne absorbed in silent prayer moves the nuns who observe her to tears.

> My companion prayed kneeling, but I lay prostrate, my forehead touching the bottom step of the altar and my arms stretching up the other steps. I don't think I have ever addressed God with more thankfulness and fervor; my heart was beating violently and in an instant I lost all awareness of my surroundings. I don't know how long I stayed in that position or how long I might have stayed in it, but I was undoubtedly a very touching spectacle for my companion and for the two nuns who had come to replace us. When I rose I thought I was alone, but I was mistaken, for the three of them were standing behind me weeping; they had not dared to interrupt me; they were waiting for me to emerge by myself from the state of elation and ecstasy in which they saw me. When I turned back toward them, the expression on my face

must have been awe-inspiring, to judge from the effect produced upon them and from what they said. (71; *147*)

The favorable response this visual tableau elicits is in sharp contrast to the negative response other images of Suzanne provoke.[2] In two specific instances, it is implied that the sight of Suzanne is so displeasing that she must be curtained off. Thus, for example, after she has publicly denied her vows, other nuns block her from sight by drawing a curtain between her and the public. In a subsequent interview with her mother, Suzanne — evidently associating the emotional displeasure she causes with the visual impact she has on others — blocks herself off from her mother's sight: "I . . . drew my hood over my face. She had put so much firmness and authority into her tone of voice that I felt I ought to conceal myself from her eyes" (34; *102*). And even the kindly Madame de Moni at one point is disturbed by the sight of Suzanne. In Suzanne's words: "One day when I was more irresolute and dejected than ever, I went to [Madame de Moni's] cell. My presence disconcerted her at first" (48; *119*). The contrast between the preceding examples and the scene of absorbed prayer again implies that Suzanne has a negative effect on others in direct face-to-face confrontations, whereas she has a positive effect when her attention is deflected elsewhere — when she prays, for instance.

A similar conclusion is implicit in Suzanne's discovery that music is an effective means of communication. Unable to convey her emotions to others when she addresses them in normal speech, Suzanne finds that she can circumvent the problem when she sings. On her first evening at Longchamp, for example, although overwhelmed by her sorrow at being forced to reenter the convent, Suzanne can find no way of expressing her grief. The superior, however, asks her to sing, a request to which Suzanne responds negatively: "My heart ached, but this was not the moment to express the repugnance I felt" (45; *115*). Her reluctance to sing presumably stems both from the overwhelming sadness she feels at finding herself once again behind the walls of a convent and from her realization that, having been accepted into this new convent because of her much-touted musical talent, she will only be sealing her unhappy fate if she sings. Nevertheless, Suzanne finally agrees to perform and, without thinking, chooses an aria by Rameau.

> I sat down at the harpsichord and improvised for a long time, searching for a piece of music in my head, which is usually full of them, but not finding any at all. However, the Superior insisted, and so, with no ulterior motive, but simply by force of habit because I knew it so well, I sang *Sad preparations, pale torches, day more terrible than darkness*. I don't know what effect that produced, but they didn't listen for long; I was interrupted by praises which I was surprised to have earned so quickly and with so little effort. (45; 115)

The lyrics and melody of the aria from Rameau's *Castor et Pollux* correspond exactly to Suzanne's current despairing state of mind. As a result, the feelings she had been unable to express directly to the superior and to the other nuns, she manages to express indirectly through a performance of someone else's music.

At a later date, Suzanne performs in a concert for the general public: "I sang, I played the organ, I was applauded" (72; 148). This time Suzanne's performance is so successful that people from the audience begin to visit her at the convent. And, whereas her previous attempts to find acceptance within society had repeatedly failed, Suzanne's musical performance allows her finally to establish contact with the outside world. Furthermore, it is not just the people on the outside but also the other nuns in the convent who are impressed with Suzanne's musical talents and with the audience's enthusiastic response. Although before her musical performance the other nuns had remained oblivious to Suzanne's entreaties for compassion, shunning her and denying her the privileges of convent life, after her success they welcome her into their ranks and restore the privileges she had been denied: "Oh, the fickleness of nuns! I hardly needed to do anything in order to be welcomed back by the whole community—they met me more than halfway" (72; *148*).

What is most interesting about both the music and the prayer scenes is Suzanne's reaction to her own performance. She does not seem to understand the message that she is transmitting; she seems to have no awareness of the effect that she is having on her audience. In fact, what she is transmitting is not a message as such, not a content, but rather affect. Suzanne's performances and silent prayers make the other nuns feel in their bones what it is like to be Suzanne at those moments, and as a result they elicit a strong response: at the end of the prayer scene, the nuns who observe Suzanne shed tears; when she finishes singing the aria from *Castor et Pollux*, they rush to comfort her; after she sings for the general public, the other nuns in the community put an end to the horrible punishments they have been inflicting on her.

Although the scenes depicting Suzanne's successes when she prays and when she sings illustrate the efficacy of indirection, there is nevertheless an important difference between the two procedures. The prayer scenes have specifically Leibnizian overtones, in the sense that all ability to communicate is mediated by God. In Leibniz's words, the "influence of one Monad upon another is only ideal, and it can have its effect only through the mediation of God."[3] Michel Serres reads this and other passages from the *Monadology* as a theory of communication: "The first known system of communication is that of Leibniz. It is both radical and simple. No one relates to anyone or anything . . . everything and everyone relates to everything else by the intermediate of God."[4] In the scene of Madame de Moni at prayer, we can see that the superior herself alludes to this triangular model of communication when, after losing her contact with God, she observes that she no longer has the same effect on her interlocutors. She even formulates this notion explicitly, telling Suzanne, "May God speak to you Himself since it does not please Him to make Himself heard through my mouth" (48; *120*). The same principle applies to the scene of Suzanne's silent prayer.

Yet Diderot's adoption of a Leibnizian model of communication whose functional premise is theological seems to be at odds with his materialist philosophy. The resemblance between Diderot's model and Leibniz's, however, is limited to the scenes that depict Madame de Moni and Suzanne at prayer, for at other points, although Diderot retains the triangular structure, he nevertheless secularizes Leibniz's model. What the music episodes show is that Leibniz's model of communication is still effective even without the theological foundation. Music, instead, takes over for God as the universal encoder, the term whose intervention facilitates communication.[5] Nowhere is this substitution more evident than in one of the most remarkable scenes of the novel, a scene whose successful outcome is of the utmost importance for Suzanne.

Having realized that her only hope of leaving the convent is to have her vows annulled in the secular courts, Suzanne secretly drafts a brief that explains the details of her case. The problem she then faces is that she must transmit her document to a lawyer in the outside world without the knowledge of the religious community that is persecuting her. Already under suspicion of trying to inform the outside world of all the terrible things that have happened to her, and realizing that her attempts to send the brief directly to a lawyer will be stopped, Suzanne decides to ask Soeur Ursule, her only friend, to act as intermediary. But a major obstacle stands in the way of her plan: the superior of the convent has placed Suzanne under constant surveillance to prevent her from having direct communication either with someone in the outside world or with another nun who could transmit a message for her to the outside. Any meeting with Soeur Ursule must therefore take place under circumstances that will not arouse anyone's suspicions. And should the opportunity to exchange information be found, it must be done in such a way that the surveillants will not overhear. In spite of these seemingly insurmountable obstacles, Suzanne manages to carry out her plan.

The singing lessons she gives provide her with the perfect alibi for meeting with Soeur Ursule. And the songs the two nuns sing during the "class" allow them to exchange information without being overheard. This is the ingenious way the exchange functions: "I sang while she spoke and she sang while I answered her, so that our conversation was broken up [*entre-coupée*] by snatches of song" (68; *143*). In this scene Suzanne creates, first of all, a visual block. What her surveillants see when they observe Suzanne and Ursule together is one nun giving the other a singing lesson and not two nuns conducting a conversation. The music in turn creates an auditory block. Because Suzanne and Ursule speak and sing simultaneously, the singing masks the spoken message for anyone within hearing range. The surveillants, therefore, can hear the songs but not the words that the two interlocutors exchange. Predictably, the strategy works. Ursule agrees to help Suzanne and successfully forwards her brief to a lawyer.

What we have in this scene is a striking illustration of dialogue as Michel Serres defines it in *La Communication*. Rejecting the traditional conception of dialogue as a binary exchange, Serres defines it instead as the product of the association of the two interlocutors, who join forces against a third term—another interlocutor or background noise—that threatens to disrupt the exchange. A dialogue "is a sort of game played by two interlocutors considered as united against the phenomena of interference and confusion, or against individuals with some stake in interrupting communication." According to Serres, the third term is at first included in the circuit of communication (when it interrupts the exchange) but subsequently excluded (when the two interlocutors join forces to overcome the interference this third term creates). In Serres's own words: "*To hold a dialogue is to suppose a third man and to seek to exclude him*; a successful communication is the exclusion of the third man."[6]

An analogous principle is at work in the dialogue between Ursule and Suzanne: music, which provides "interferential" noise, permits the exchange of information. But Diderot's model is more complicated than Serres's, since music, Diderot's third term, not only facilitates the exchange between Suzanne and Ursule but also prevents a third group of interlocutors from having access to it.

However, although music creates the interference that prevents Suzanne's surveillants from overhearing the conversation between the two nuns, no such interference exists for the reader. Suzanne merely describes the stratagem she employs against the surveillants. What the reader witnesses on the printed page, however, is the complete text of the exchange. The musical conversation thus grants the reader privileged access to a secret exchange, thereby defining the reader's position with respect to the fictional universe as that of an insider. Like the "letter that was never sent" in the *Préface-annexe*, the dialogue between Ursule and Suzanne functions as a point of insertion for the reader, creating a complicitous possessor of information unavailable to the characters in the fiction. Thus the exclusion of this third group of interlocutors paradoxically facilitates the inclusion of a fourth: the reader of the novel.

This is not just a passive inclusion. Besides giving the reader privileged access to the content of the conversation between Ursule and Suzanne, this scene gives the reader a small but active role in the development of its narrative texture. For music — the noise against which the conversation takes shape — cannot be represented *textually*. Therefore, although Suzanne states that "our conversation was broken up [*entrecoupée*] by snatches of song," the full complexity of the exchange, including the musical *entrecoupage*, can be performed only by the reader, who must imagine the "snatches of song" that are supposed to be an integral part of the dialogue.

The musical conversation therefore functions according to the same principle as the epistolary exchange in the *Préface-annexe*: as we saw, the bifurcating, outwardly expanding circuit of communication ultimately serves to incorporate the reader as one of its terms. This dialogue functions, in other words, not just as a thematic illustration of Diderot's mechanism for indirect communication but also as the structure of the relationship that the text maintains with its reader.

Suzanne embodies this structuring principle. In her role as narrator, she creates obstacles for the reader that he has to fight to overcome and that as a consequence actively involve him with the text. The overcoming of obstacles thus becomes a means of drawing the reader in. One such instance appears in the ambiguous remark she offers as an explanation of the cruelty implicit in the phrase *Requiescat in pace*, a phrase that Suzanne's fellow nuns utter one by one at the end of the mock funeral they force her to undergo. Besides betraying the nuns' cruel desire for Suzanne's death, the words reveal an antagonistic wish of a subtler sort: "You have to be familiar with the language of convents in order to appreciate the particular threat implied in those . . . words" (81; 159), says Suzanne. But although she alludes to some sort of threat, she never states explicitly what that threat is.

Modern readers, of course, have access to scholarly footnotes that provide the missing information: the *in-pace* is a cell in which disobedient nuns are imprisoned. Without the benefit of such footnotes, however, the reader finds himself in one of two positions. If the reader does know the meaning of the words, Suzanne's refusal to provide a full translation puts the reader in a position in which he must provide the missing information, thereby incorporating him into the elaboration of the fiction. If he does not know the specialized meaning of *Requiescat in pace*, the phrase remains ambiguous for him. This ambiguity leads to the reader's partial exclusion, which paradoxically is designed to produce his eventual inclusion. For the very ambiguity of the phrase operates a subtle seduction, providing an incentive for the reader to delve further into the fiction in the hope of deciphering "the language of convents."

In both instances, however, it is neither the clarity nor the completeness of Suzanne's message that accounts for its strategic efficacy. Roland Barthes provides an explanation of the functional premises of this paradox in a passage from *S/Z* in which he analyzes the strategy of the double entendre.

> In relation to an ideally pure message . . . the division of reception constitutes a "noise," it makes communication obscure . . . uncertain. Yet this noise, this uncertainty are emitted by the discourse with a view toward a communication . . . what the reader consumes is this defect in communication, this deficient message . . . the reader is an accomplice, not of this or that character, but of the discourse itself insofar as it plays on the . . . impurity of communication.[7]

What this passage makes evident is not only that the model of communication through interference appears in *La Religieuse* on the thematic level but also that, as employed by Suzanne, it becomes a part of Diderot's narrative strategy. Her withholding of information introduces "noise" into the circuit of communication between text and reader, noise that does not disrupt the interaction between text and reader but rather grants the reader a more active role in the production of meaning.

THE UNDOING OF RETROSPECTIVE NARRATION

Conventional first-person retrospective narration presupposes the narrator's knowledge of the ultimate consequences of his or her life.[8] This mode of narration is characteristic of the autobiographical or memoir-novel, in which the narrator recounts a series of events in his or her life only after knowing the outcome. Those critics who claim that *La Religieuse* is a memoir-novel and therefore assume that it is narrated from a retrospective vantage point are often disturbed to discover that Suzanne's mode of narration deviates from the conventional model. Instead of acknowledging her awareness of the meaning of certain key events in her life, Suzanne in fact systematically blocks it out. Various critics have therefore concluded that Diderot somehow lost sight of the structural coherence of his novel and the conventions of the genre in which he was writing.[9] I would argue, on the contrary, that Diderot employs these so-called lapses from convention for a specific reason, a reason that bears out the theoretical program for literary discourse of the *Préface-annexe*. But to clarify this point, we must first examine the peculiarities of Suzanne's narration.

Suzanne specifically blocks out her knowledge of sexuality, a knowledge acquired not, as might be expected, outside the convent but rather during her years there. When Suzanne first entered the convent, she was sexually innocent. Unaware even of the existence of homosexuality, her experiences in the convent disabuse her. By the time she decides to escape from her last convent, Suzanne has learned that two women can indeed have sexual relations, and specifically that the mother superior of that convent is a lesbian who, unbeknownst to Suzanne, has made more than one attempt to seduce her. Her knowledge is evident from her admission, toward the end of the narrative, that she had listened to the superior's confession through a keyhole. But Suzanne subsequently seems to "forget" what she has learned, as several moments in her narrative reveal.

When, for example, the community of nuns accuses her of having sexual designs on one of its members, she says: "Of course I am not a man, and I don't know what can be imagined about one woman and another . . . and so I have never quite understood what they accused me of" (86; *164*). And, in another instance, Suzanne describes the mother superior's visit to her cell on her first night at the convent of St. Eutrope in the following way.

> On the first evening I was visited by the Superior, who came to my formal undressing. It was she who took off my veil and wimple and who arranged my hair for the night; it was she who undressed me. She said a hundred sweet nothings to me and lavished on me a thousand caresses that embarrassed me a little, why I don't know, for I did not understand what was happening and neither did she. And even now, when I think back to it, what could we have understood? (126; *214*)

This passage presents more than a simple case of bad faith, for in it Suzanne not only insists that at the time of this encounter with her superior she could not understand the implications of the superior's actions but also claims that the superior did not understand them. She then claims that even in the present, at the very moment she is recounting the event, she continues to be unaware of its sexual connotations. These claims, needless to say, are totally implausible, because by the time Suzanne begins to narrate the event in question, she has already acquired the knowledge that would allow her to interpret its significance. Nor are the two preceding examples the only instances of Suzanne's strange blindness to sexuality. Throughout the novel, she repeatedly asserts, against all logic, that she has retained her innocence. The important question here, of course, is why Diderot chose to defy narrative logic in this way, a question that has troubled numerous critics of *La Religieuse*.

Some have attributed Diderot's flawed narrative logic to his haste in composing the text.[10] Others have argued that the "flaws" are a result of Diderot's alleged capacity to identify with the characters he portrays, to the point that he forgets that they are imaginary.[11] Whether Diderot drafted *La Religieuse* in too much of a hurry and whether he unconsciously identified with Suzanne while he was writing obviously remain open to question, but it is interesting to note once more how effectively the *Préface-annexe* prepares the reader for the novel that follows. It is as if the myth of Diderot's "sensibility," whose source is in large part the *Préface-annexe* itself, were capable of attenuating the resistance of readers to the novel's logical inconsistencies, thereby allowing them to accept these unsettling "flaws" as another manifestation of a distinctive "trait" of Diderot's psychology.

In their recent edition of *La Religieuse*, however, Georges May and Herbert Dieckmann provide evidence that undermines the force of previous attempts to explain away the "flaws" in Suzanne's narrative. May points out that Diderot added two of Suzanne's most notoriously illogical protestations of innocence when he revised the 1760 version of *La Religieuse* in 1780–81.[12] The twenty-year lapse between the moment when Diderot drafted the first versions of *La Religieuse* and the moment when he added the new passages might lead one to conclude that Diderot had lost sight of the exigencies of retrospective narration in the novel as a whole by the time he undertook his revisions. However, Dieckmann notes that "few are the works that Diderot corrected as carefully as he did *La Religieuse*."[13] The fact that Diderot corrected the original manuscript of *La Religieuse* with such care—and while so doing added some of the passages that have troubled many critics of the novel—points to the conclusion that the so-called inconsistencies in Suzanne's narrative should not be considered a result of mere inadvertence on Diderot's part but ought rather to be seen as a distinctive and intentional feature of the narrative.[14] Instead of questioning Diderot's control of his craft, therefore, let us instead suppose that the alleged inadvertences in the narrative fulfill a specific purpose.

What such a purpose might be begins to emerge if we consider the relationship between text and reader that Suzanne's deviant strategy activates. In conventional retrospective narration, the narrator exercises a certain mastery over the reader: he or she knows something that is not revealed to the reader until the end of the narrative. Suzanne, on the contrary, divests herself of any such pretension to mastery; she continually suppresses the moment of realization that comes at the end of her stay in the convent, the moment when the "truth" of her experiences is revealed to her. What she does as a narrator, in other words, is to adopt the vantage point of the reader as he reads, for the reader can have no knowledge of the outcome of the events in Suzanne's life until he reaches the end of the novel. The blocks Suzanne creates and maintains in her narrating "consciousness"—which produce "flaws" in the narrative logic—paradoxically take on a positive narrative function. They create another point of insertion for the reader, narrowing the distance between him and the narrator by positioning both within the same vantage point relative to the progression of events in the narrative.

Although this might lead us to conclude that the narrator and the reader each know only as much as the other at any given point, in fact the interaction between text and reader that Suzanne's narrative strategy generates is more complex. There are times when the reader knows more than the narrator. At the moments when Suzanne participates in activities whose erotic connotations she denies, she nevertheless provides minute descriptions of their explicitly sexual aspects, including physiological reactions. The implicit assumption at these moments, therefore, is that the reader is less naive than Suzanne and consequently understands more than she does about the significance of her actions. As a result, Suzanne's lapses establish a complicity between the author and the reader; both know more than the narrator about her situation. This seems to be one way in which Diderot demystifies the naive identification of the author of a text with its narrator.

Thus, at the same time that Diderot creates a similitude in the positioning of the narrator and the reader by means of Suzanne's peculiar narrative strategy, he demystifies this strategy by distancing the reader from Suzanne's current interpretation of the events in her life. Suzanne's special brand of first-person narration is, therefore, at once a mechanism designed to establish an identity between the reader's perspective and the narrator's perspective and, paradoxically, the element that creates a distance between them. This last point seems to contradict my claim that Diderot continually attempts to draw the reader into the fiction. But the apparent distance he creates between narrator and reader can be construed instead to corroborate my claim. Although Suzanne supposedly experiences convent life from the inside, she in fact remains on the outside. Her militant innocence prevents her from having an insider's view of convent life; she remains blind to its realities until the very end of her account. It is the reader, instead, who, as a result, has the insider's view.

This is not to say, however, that Diderot here grants the reader mastery over the narrator. Instead he destabilizes the position of both. Unlike a conventional retrospective narrator, who accedes to a stable and totalizing vantage point from which he or she can see, know, and evaluate the significance of all the previous events in his or her life, Suzanne's innocence prevents her from ever attaining such a vantage point. What the lacunae in her narrating "consciousness" reveal is that as a narrator she has only partial knowledge of the events she recounts and not a privileged perspective on them. This is a generalized phenomenon. These lapses in her awareness occur not only in the scenes depicting sexual encounters but also at other points in the narrative. Suzanne repeatedly draws attention to her inability to remember key events in her life. During her vow-taking ceremony, for example, she is unaware of everything that takes place around her and subsequently cannot remember what she said or did: "Others disposed of me all through that morning, which was nonexistent in my life, for I never knew how long it lasted, what I did or what I said. Presumably I was questioned, presumably I replied. I pronounced vows, but I have no recollection of them" (51; *123–24*).

Suzanne's lapses, which the reader can identify as such and of which he is constantly reminded, in turn destabilize his position, for the reader's only access to information about events in the fictional universe is through Suzanne, a narrator who herself does not have a firm vantage point on them. What the lapses in her memory and in her awareness reveal is that the reader's understanding is built on extremely shaky foundations. Both the reader's and the narrator's positions, therefore, prove to be unstable.

As for the relationship between the reader, the narrator, and the universe of the fiction, here too there is a ternary circuit of communication, with the narrator functioning as the third term in the circuit. But because the narrator is in an unstable position, the conditions that exist for communication—from the reader's perspective—are no longer optimal, as they were, for example, in the musical conversation between Ursule and Suzanne in which the absence of interference for the reader granted him privileged access to the content of the conversation between the two nuns. What Suzanne's unconventional mode of retrospective narration accomplishes is precisely the opposite. Her innocence creates interference for the reader. But the interference does not render the circuit dysfunctional. Rather, it functions like background noise, at first seeming to mask the message but instead not only facilitating the message but in the most important cases actually generating it. As we saw earlier, the interference that Suzanne's innocence creates makes the reader necessary to the generation of the narrative; it is the reader who imaginatively reconstructs and fills in information that Suzanne leaves out. In fact we can go so far as to claim that the narrative is constituted in the detour it must take through the reader.

The destabilization of the ternary model of communication seems to have subversive epistemological and political implications. To return for a moment to the Leibnizian model referred to earlier, we can see that its stability is provided by the crucial third term, God. In this instance, God is in a position that allows a totalizing view and knowledge of the monads, and therefore he can wield absolute power over them. This vantage point is homologous to that of the conventional retrospective narrator and also to that of the king in a monarchy. In moving from a stable ternary model to an unstable one, therefore, Diderot seems to be undoing the conservative political and epistemological implications of the Leibnizian model. He does this, however, not merely by equalizing all the terms of the system but rather by unbalancing them, destabilizing their positions, and thereby putting them into a constant movement that prevents any one term from being valorized over the other.

This sort of destabilization marks the change from a spatial to a temporal model. The Leibnizian model of communication described above is a spatial model, which Diderot at first adopts (in the prayer scene with Madame de Moni) and subsequently secularizes (in the conversation between Ursule and Suzanne, in which he omits God altogether). The key term here is "secular," which has a double acceptation. It means, on the one hand, "not specifically pertaining to religion or to a religious body" and, on the other, "pertaining to the temporal rather than to the spiritual." In the scene of the musical conversation between Ursule and Suzanne, in which the theological model was first secularized, we can see the beginnings of the shift from the spatial to the temporal model.

Let us reconsider the sentence with which Suzanne describes the structure of the conversation with Ursule: "I sang while she spoke and she sang while I answered her, so that our conversation was broken up [*entrecoupée*] by snatches of song" (68; *143*). There is a tension in this sentence between the simultaneity implicit in the spatial model and the succession implicit in a temporal model. The simultaneity of the various actions the nuns must perform (one must speak while the other *both* listens and sings) is expressed in the first part of the sentence with the conjunction "while," whereas succession is expressed in the second part of the sentence with the term *entrecoupée*, which, according to Robert, means "repeatedly interrupted."[15] The factor that creates an imbalance between these two terms, which at first appear to be equally balanced, is the reader, who breaks up the simultaneity of the representation into an imagined temporal succession. Thus the detour via the reader, necessary to the development of the narrative, in turn introduces narrativized time. This point requires further elaboration.

The conventional model of retrospective narration is spatial, since it is constituted by the totalizing, external vantage point that the retrospective narrator is supposed to possess. Diderot destabilizes this model by eliminating such a vantage point from Suzanne's narration. The destabilization of the spatial model thus generates the temporal model of narration, a model that mimics the real complexity of the experience of the passage of time. To understand how this happens, it is necessary to explore the effects that Suzanne's suppression of knowledge have on the temporal structure of her narrative.

THE TEMPORAL MODEL OF NARRATION

Critics have often commented on the temporal "inconsistencies" that recur throughout *La Religieuse*.[16] One well-known example is the problem of Suzanne's age. Although the novel covers a time span of approximately nine years, and although Suzanne is supposed to be sixteen and a half years old when the novel begins, toward the end of her account she states that she is not yet twenty. And it is not just at this point that her own appraisal of her age is inconsistent with the internal chronology of the novel. Throughout her narrative, Suzanne consistently underestimates her age. As a result, she appears not to grow older but instead to resist the passage of time.

Another of *La Religieuse*'s famous temporal "blunders" appears in the letter Suzanne's mother writes to her daughter shortly before dying. In this letter, Madame Simonin informs Suzanne that she is sending her a package containing some money along with the letter. But she formulates this statement in the following way: "The person to whom I am entrusting this money had come the day before, and I had given him this little package, with this letter, which he has written to my dictation" (54; *127*). The problem here is obvious: How could she have mailed yesterday the letter that continues today?[17]

But there are other deformations of narrative temporality in *La Religieuse* that are specifically the product of Suzanne's constant suppression of knowledge. At the very beginning of her account, for instance, Suzanne states that "My father . . . had three daughters" (21; 82), although by the time she "writes" this phrase she knows (1) that M. Simonin is not her father and hence (2) that in fact he only had two daughters. Moreover, she does not accompany the preceding statement with any of the anticipatory warnings or foreshadowings (such as "If only I had known then") typical of retrospective narration. It is not until she arrives at the point in her narrative that coincides with the beginnings of her own suspicions about the circumstances of her birth that the reader has any inkling of Suzanne's illegitimacy.

Textually, this deformation of the temporality characteristic of retrospective narration is reflected at various times in Suzanne's inappropriate use of the present tense, which, as

Georges May notes, cannot always be explained away as instances of the historical present. Citing Suzanne's aberrant use of the present tense in her portrait of Father Lemoine, for example, May writes: "Certain . . . instances of the present tense are tantamount to real blunders, and notably the following: 'in his monastery he is reputed to be a great theologian.' Several pages later we learn, in fact, that Father Lemoine had been replaced by another priest because he was suspected of having 'advanced views.' "[18] The ambiguous status of the past in Suzanne's narrative is also reflected in her inconsistent and constantly shifting use of past tenses. As Philip Stewart notes, Suzanne slips "from *passé simple* to imperfect tense and vice versa. Properly applied, such a transition can be part of a normal technique. . . . But in this novel, and particularly in the scenes depicting Sainte-Eutrope, narrative time seems to become very obscure."[19]

Jumbled chronology, therefore, is strangely enough the corollary of the real-time chronology that Suzanne's suppression of knowledge implicitly creates. This suggests, first of all, a link between the odd temporality of *La Religieuse* and the relationship between reader and text that this novel activates. Such deviations from the norms of retrospective narration, curiously enough, create a different notion of order for the reader: they allow him to follow the unfolding of the events in the narrator's life in a perfectly linear chronological sequence, the same sequence in which Suzanne originally experienced those events. However, Suzanne's narration is a peculiarly uncomfortable one, for she is unable to make clear distinctions between past and present. Instead she conflates them to form a kind of continuous present, an impossible real-time narration. To understand how this can be so, however, it will first be necessary to explore the notion of temporality that informs classic retrospective narration, a notion that I shall call "reversible time."

Reversibility is a notion derived from the mathematical description of scientific laws in Newtonian mechanics. According to this theory of the functioning of nature, the primary relationship between events in the natural world is that of cause and effect. A law is therefore defined as the generalization of a particular cause-and-effect relationship. That relationship, moreover, can be read in either direction: from the cause to the effect or from the effect to the cause. Reversibility thus refers to the way one can read the relationship between events and not to whether the events themselves can be reversed. It is a question of interpretive procedures; in such a world, one uses the same procedures to explain the past or predict the future.

Reversible time is the time that is traditionally associated with retrospective narration. In order to recount the story of his or her life, the narrator turns back the clock and moves from the present through the past. The narrator's act of narrating is located in the present, but the content of the narration is events — actions — located in the past. That content is recognizable as content and generates meaning only if it is marked as past in relation to the vantage point of the interpreting present, for the narrator's present vantage point allows him or her to perceive the causal links between the events in his or her past.

Like the reversible narrator, Suzanne's narrative indeed contains past events, but she speaks about them as though they were present events. She therefore deviates from the model of reversible temporal narration when she refuses to distinguish between past and present. In so doing, furthermore, she turns her past into her present and shifts from "reversible" narration to what we might call by analogy "irreversible" narration. Her act of narration, rather than maintaining a judgmental vantage point on the content of the narration, coincides with it. Therefore the point of closure that exists in any reversible narration—the moment where past and present meet up and everything becomes clear—cannot occur in Suzanne's narrative.

The doubled perspective characteristic of the writer of a reversible text results from the writer's need to provide an *explanation* of the events in his or her life. The writer has to recount those events not only as the person who lived them but also as the person who judges the relationship between them. However, as we have already seen, this is precisely what Suzanne does not do; she recounts her tale without understanding herself or the implications of most of her actions. But this is not to say that Suzanne never acquires the understanding that she has lacked all along; she finally does acquire it, but only *after* she has finished drafting her text. This is what the curious postscript tacked on to the end of her narrative reveals.

> P.S. I am overwhelmed with fatigue, surrounded by terrors, and unable to sleep. These memoirs, which I wrote in haste, I have just reread at leisure, and I have realized that without the slightest intention I had shown myself in every line to be certainly as unhappy as I was, but much more likable than I am. Could it be that we think men are less affected by a picture of our troubles than by a portrait of our charms? And do we count on its being easier to seduce them than to touch their hearts? I know them too little, and I haven't studied myself enough to know. And yet supposing the Marquis, who is reputed to be the most delicate of men, were to persuade himself that I am addressing myself not to his best instincts but to his worst, what would he think of me? This thought worries me. In truth he would be quite mistaken if he ascribed to me personally an instinct belonging to all my sex. I am a woman, and perhaps a bit coquettish—Who can tell?—but only naturally so and without artifice.   (188–89; 288)

"These memoirs, which I wrote in haste, I have just reread at leisure." What does Suzanne mean when she says that she wrote her memoirs in haste? Was she trying to complete them before a deadline? The answer to this question is very obviously no. Suzanne's haste is not a function of external events or pressures, as we are immediately shown by the opposition that Diderot sets up between the phrases "in haste" and "at leisure": she writes "in haste" and reads "at leisure." Rather, her haste is a function of an internal state, a sign of urgency, of emotional investment or, to use Michael Fried's term, of her total "absorption" in the process of recounting her past life. Indeed her absorption is such that Suzanne writes her memoirs as if she were reliving the events she recounts, because effectively she is reliving them (as we saw, to cite just one instance, when she said that even during her act of narration she did not understand the implications of the lesbian mother superior's actions). Suzanne is not writing her narrative with any consciousness of the link between the events in her life; in other words, she is not writing from the vantage point of a judge. She does not therefore construct a reversible narrative; it is instead left up to the reader to deduce the cause-and-effect links between events.

Yet the initial effect of this process on the reader is not the predictable one. The reader's reconstruction of the cause-and-effect links does not at first allow him to make sense of the events in Suzanne's life. Instead the initial result is that the reader becomes aware of how unaware Suzanne is of whatever is happening around her or, in other words, of how absorbed she is. The writing of her memoirs, because all of it was done "in haste," is therefore an event of the same kind as the absorptive events (the silent prayer scene, the musical performances, etc.) that Suzanne depicts within them. We know that while Suzanne writes she is absorbed beyond the point of reason, because Madame Madin chronicles in great detail the effect that this activity has upon her. Indeed Madame Madin makes it clear that it is Suzanne's writing and not her illness that is killing her: "I begged her to show me what she had written. . . . This, I said to her angrily, is precisely what is killing you" (59).

The doctor concurs in this opinion and, along with Madame Madin, forbids Suzanne to write any more: "I forbade her to continue [writing]; her doctor did also" (59).

Suzanne's absorption, her prayer to the Marquis de Croismare, in turn has a profound effect on the structure of her narrative. Indeed Suzanne's narrative becomes more and more true to life—more fragmentary and immediate and less smoothed out by judgmental hindsight—the more absorbed she becomes in the writing and the closer she approaches the actual moment of narration. In contrast to the reversible text, which begins with fragmented facts and builds to a clear conceptual unity, Suzanne's text begins with the smoothness resulting from the control available to a cool head (the state in which she began) and then starts to undo itself, for the more absorbed she is, the more disjointed her narrative becomes. First the order of exposition breaks down and eventually, after the point at which she leaves the convent, even its structure fragments.

Suzanne's absorption also results in a dissociation of two functions that usually go together in conventional retrospective narration. As we noted earlier, the narrator of a retrospective text recounts events in the past not only as the person who lived through them, but also as the person who judges the relationship between those events or, to put this another way, as the person who reads them. The retrospective narrator, in other words, is both a writer and a reader at the same time.

Suzanne, however, does not follow this pattern. First she recounts her story, and only afterwards does the interpretive work that she had omitted from her narrative. I would posit that this is the source of the inconsistencies in Suzanne's narrative. While she is in the process of writing her life story, she is able to look at herself only directly, as if the text were her mirror. According to the terms of the model of indirect communication, she is therefore doomed at every turn not to be able to understand. It is only at the point when she reads her memoirs "at leisure," or in other words, at the moment when she adopts the position of a conventional reader, that Suzanne acquires the understanding that she was lacking before. What she then discovers through her reading—and she is finally able to make it very clear, although she does so elliptically—is that she herself has been seduced by her own text. Up until this experience, Suzanne claims that "I haven't studied myself enough to know [how to seduce]" and that she had therefore written her memoirs without the least intention of being seductive. It is in the reading of her text that she has to recognize that it is nevertheless a paradigm of seduction. Her answer to this "thought" that "worries" her is that seductiveness must have creeped into her text because she is "a bit coquettish . . . but only naturally so and without artifice," which is to say that her text is seductive because she wrote it in an absorbed state of mind ("without artifice") that prevented her from reflecting and therefore constructing a reversible text. At this point Suzanne becomes her own best witness both of the nature of the text as seductive and of the effect it has on its reader. She has finally gained the awareness that she had lacked all along. Through overcoming the many obstacles in her own text, Suzanne is finally able to communicate with herself—and therefore understand herself—indirectly.

My reading of the postscript departs from the traditional one, which sees this text as the final proof of Suzanne's bad faith. However, if we let ourselves be guided by the reader-writer relationships revealed in the *Préface-annexe* and take the postscript at face value, then a different reading emerges. The postscript allows us to identify a fundamental difference between the traditional reversible text and Suzanne's absorptive or affective text. Whereas in the former the narrator-function and the reader-function coincide, in the latter they are fully dissociated. It follows, then, that it may not be necessary to read this passage ironically. If we read it literally instead, as Suzanne finally becoming the reader of her own text, it explains the peculiarities of the narrative structure of *La Religieuse*. To show why Diderot would do something like this in the novel that he claimed as his favorite, let us look for support in another famous text: *Jacques le fataliste*.

THE INTERRUPTION IS THE MESSAGE

Whereas *La Religieuse* implicitly works within the framework of a set of literary conventions while undermining them by pointedly diverging from them, in *Jacques le fataliste* we enter a world where virtually every assumption about narrative art and its conventions has already been exploded and therefore is no longer at issue.[20] No longer classifiable within traditional categories of genre, no longer following any conventional narrative pattern, *Jacques le fataliste*, as the "author"-narrator repeatedly reminds us, "is not a novel."[21] Although it may not be a novel in any conventional sense of the term, *Jacques* marks a final step in the development of Diderot's program for fiction and provides additional corroboration of my claims. The principal elements of this program reappear in *Jacques*, but instead of remaining implicit, as they had in the earlier works, they are now explicitly thematized.

This is the case, for example, of the model of indirect communication. In *Jacques* it makes a striking reappearance during the conversation among the hostess of the Inn of the Grand-Cerf, Jacques, and the master. In the same way that music both interfered with and facilitated the transmission of the message in the musical conversation between Suzanne and Ursule, in the conversation in *Jacques* noise both interrupts and facilitates communication.[22]

Jacques's function in the conversation is unusual, however, for he is not only a term in the circuit of communication but also the source of the noise, since he constantly interrupts the hostess and distracts her from her narrative. True to the model, although at first noise (Jacques's interruptions) is included in the circuit, subsequently the hostess and the master join forces to exclude it: "To resume the interrupted story . . . the only condition [the hostess] imposed was that Jacques shut up. His master promised silence on behalf of Jacques" (106; *120*). And the exclusion of Jacques in turn creates a bond between the hostess and the master, as the hostess subsequently reveals when she pointedly addresses her narrative solely to "Monsieur" (107; *121*) (to the master and not to Jacques, in other words) and when she explicitly informs Jacques that she is not speaking to him (107; *121*). The master, in turn, acknowledges the complicity between them by using sign language to indicate that Jacques is crazy, a language that the hostess has no trouble understanding and to which she responds in kind: "His master made a sign to the innkeeper's wife which led her to understand that Jacques's brain was a little scrambled. She replied to the master's sign with a sympathetic movement of the shoulders and added: 'At his age. What a terrible shame'" (107; *122*).

At this point, however, the scene takes a parodic turn. Jacques, who is not happy to be excluded from the exchange, again interrupts the hostess, turning the tables on her and using her own strategy of exclusion against her. When she reprimands him with the words "Monsieur Jacques, you're interrupting me," he retorts: "Madame, hostess of the Grand-Cerf, I'm not talking to you" (107; *122*).

This exchange is taking place, however, against another sort of background noise that constantly interrupts it, namely, the noise emanating from other rooms in the inn (the hostess hears her dog moaning at one point and breaks off her narrative) and from the servants, who constantly ask the hostess for instructions:

"Madame!"
"What is it?"
"The key to the oat bin?"
"See if it's on the nail. If it's not there look in the lock." (108; 123)

The hostess, tired of having her story continually interrupted, tries on more than one occasion to put an end to the disturbances, but to no avail. Here again, it seems that the hostess misunderstands the function of these interruptions in her narrative, for she sees them as having a negative rather than a positive value. Jacques and the master, on the other hand, understand their positive function. Both admit that their interest in the hostess's story has been sharpened by the constant interruptions:

> MASTER This woman tells a story much better than an innkeeper's wife ought to.
> JACQUES That is true. The constant interruptions from the people of the house made me feel impatient several times.
> MASTER And me too. (113; 128)

Subsequently Jacques, as if to intensify his own interest by indulging in the pleasure of interruption, takes it upon himself to interrupt the hostess's story again: "Jacques, who had begun to get interested, said to their hostess: 'Perhaps if we were to drink to the health of Madame de La Pommeraye?'" (122; 140).

Thus the constant interference of background noise in the hostess's tale ultimately facilitates communication, creating suspense for the listeners and, in addition, creating a bond among all the interlocutors, a bond that did not exist before the interruptions threatened to disrupt the hostess's story altogether. Jacques, upon seeing that the hostess was about to usurp his role as raconteur, had petulantly declared that he was not interested in her story. As we saw earlier, the hostess herself had deliberately excluded Jacques from participation in the exchange. But the repeated threats to the continuation of her narrative change all this and unite all the interlocutors in the common goal of pushing the story to its end.

If we consider the whole narrative of *Jacques le fataliste*, we can see that the innkeeper's scene manifests locally a pattern that can be traced globally in the novel. Interruption functions in *Jacques le fataliste* as the factor that generates narrative instead of disrupting it: it sustains interest. To understand this paradox, however, we must first examine the issue of the story of Jacques's loves.

Throughout *Jacques le fataliste*, the master, Jacques, and the "author"-narrator posit that the story of Jacques's amorous adventures is the novel's primary narrative line. It is the story with which the novel begins and to which the characters constantly allude. Whenever the subject of the narrative changes, one of the characters invariably points out that the story of Jacques's loves is being set aside. At such moments, for instance, the "narrator" often intervenes to anticipate the reader's question: "I can hear you, Reader, you are asking me: 'What about the story of Jacques's loves?'" (164; *189*). And Jacques himself complains about the master's constant questions, pointing out that to answer them he must inevitably stray from the "principal" topic (53; 60). Despite his complaints about the master's interruptions, however, Jacques is also often guilty of interrupting the flow of his own narrative and therefore must be constantly reminded by his master: "Well now, Jacques, the story of your loves?" (31; *35*).

Notwithstanding the insistence with which the master, Jacques, and the "author"-narrator call for the resumption of the tale of Jacques's loves, as the novel progresses it becomes increasingly evident that Jacques's amorous adventures are far from being the primary thread of the narrative. The master, Jacques, and the "author"-narrator are not the exclusive source of the relentless interruptions of Jacques's account. Other characters they encounter along the way—in addition to fortuitous events such as natural calamities, rebellious horses, and so forth—also disrupt the telling of Jacques's tale. Interestingly enough, in more than one instance, a noise is literally the cause of the interruption. In the middle of one of Jacques's tales about his captain, for example: "At this point they heard a lot of noise and shouting coming from some distance behind them. They looked back and saw a band of men armed with sticks and forks coming toward them as fast as they could run" (30; 34). Or as again many pages later, when Jacques attempts to tell the story of his captain's life: "Jacques was on the point of beginning his captain's story when they heard a large number of men and horses coming up behind them" (62; 71). The interruptions produce either a new adventure (with the intrusion of unforeseen events in which Jacques and/or the master participate and whose description becomes part of the narrative) or the telling of a different tale (with the inclusion of a character who takes over the function of narrator and recounts a story that bears no relation to the story of Jacques's loves). It is, in other words, a narrative generated by the detours it takes from what at first appears to be its primary story line.

Up to this point, our analysis of the structure of *Jacques le fataliste* is consistent with the model of indirect communication previously traced in *La Religieuse*. But *Jacques le fataliste* takes the model one step further and begins to undo it, for it undermines the possibility of making a distinction between what constitutes a "message" and what constitutes "noise." Although at first the interruptions in the telling of Jacques's tale appear to be the noise and the story of Jacques's loves appears to be the message, the interruptions are so numerous and so productive that they make such a distinction seem senseless.

Indeed Jacques's tale seems to exist for the sole purpose of being interrupted, for it is the interruptions and not the history of Jacques's loves that generate the actual narrative continuity of *Jacques le fataliste*. Indeed Jacques's history is the one story in the novel that, although begun innumerable times, is barely advanced with each new beginning and, in the last analysis, is never told. The story of Jacques's amorous adventures therefore might just as well be designated the noise that interrupts the actual narrative—the message—of the novel, since this story provides the background interference in the narrative structure against which the stories that are in fact told in the novel take shape. And, like the other instances of noise examined previously, the story of Jacques's loves becomes a point of contact, the crucial third term that allows the circuit of communication to be maintained not just between Jacques and the master, but also between the "author" and the reader, all of whom supposedly feel the same urgency to arrive at the end of Jacques's story. Thus *Jacques le fataliste* ultimately equates the categories of noise and message, thereby putting the status of each into question.

Understanding the nature of this urgency as the real message of the novel finally allows us to deal with the end of *La Religieuse*. Seduction is the message of *La Religieuse*: it is the continuity of the reader's interest that is at stake here and not the logic of the story. Urgency, in other words, defines the irreversible text. It is irreversible because it becomes impossible to stop while writing or reading such a text. One does not pause to say, "It does not make sense." That issue becomes inconsequential because it is irrelevant to the affect that Suzanne gets her dates wrong, that she never seems to age, and that her mother's letter was completed after it was mailed. On the contrary, all of these logical inconsistencies, rather than pushing the reader out of the text, contribute to the almost unbearable feeling of immediacy that is precisely the response Diderot wishes to provoke in the reader. Indeed the logical inconsistencies serve a distinct purpose. They are not supposed to explain, they are not even supposed to *be touching* (a process that, as Diderot defines it in other texts, and as we shall specifically see in the *Rêve de d'Alembert*, can potentially lead to understanding and therefore to the reader's regaining some form of conceptual control). They are instead supposed to *seduce*. The reader is totally at their mercy.

We are now in a position to understand the narrative lessons of *La Religieuse*: narrative is process, a process of generating an urgent reading experience. This point allows us to return to our initial question: Would it not be possible to raise objections to the preceding arguments since so many critics have nonetheless objected to the "illogical" temporality and to the narrative "blunders" in *La Religieuse*? Such objections, however, do not take into account the experience of reading that *La Religieuse* generates. The same critics who object to the logical and temporal inconsistencies in *La Religieuse* also claim that it is a "realist" novel and praise it for its capacity to create an illusion of reality. Speculating on the reasons for this apparent impossibility, Georges May remarks: "None of the awkwardnesses of composition, none of the patent errors Diderot made and that we pointed out earlier, is revealed on a *first reading* of *La Religieuse: as it progresses, the action sweeps along the reader's conviction*" (my emphasis).[23]

May's description of his own experience of reading supports our answer to the question of why the novel so effectively creates the illusion of reality *despite* its built-in errors. It implies that Diderot was counting on the dynamism of the reading process to transform what might otherwise be considered elements incompatible with temporal and narrative logic into elements that become perfectly compatible during the experience of reading.

Thus, in *La Religieuse*, Diderot thematizes processes that do not function according to conventional rationalist premises, processes that defy the rules of logic, processes in which noise is defined as the condition that makes possible the system rather than a dysfunction, narrative processes that depend on the narrator's repressing the knowledge she possesses of her own life experience and which therefore reveal her psychological inconsistency, and so forth. But the real tour de force of *La Religieuse* is that in the experience of reading, it overcomes the rationalist prejudices of readers and changes their intellectual perspective, allowing them to sense the viability of the nonrationalist viewpoint that it proposes. In other words, the process of narrating itself creates a displacement vis-à-vis the content of what is being narrated. It does so by displacing the displacement onto the reader.

It is often assumed that the reader's ability to overlook the flaws in the narrative can result only from the novelist's effective concealment of narrative artifices: "The goal of the writer of realist novels can therefore only be to conceal his artifices and techniques or, more precisely, to prevent the reader from noticing them. In order to do this, it is sufficient to prevent the reader from stopping to think or, in other words, to maintain his interest."[24] In this example, Georges May posits that only the critic, after having once read the text and experienced its transformational impact, can then go back and see the tricks in the narrative. But, as we saw earlier in the *Préface-annexe* — and given the additional evidence that *La Religieuse* provides — this view does not take into account the complex interaction between text and reader that Diderot's narrative generates, for Diderot assumes that the reader will both notice the inconsistencies and be able to figure out why they do not undermine the text. Diderot understood what critics frequently do not, namely that, in Serres's words, there is no thought "without error," no communication "without static," that in fact "mistakes . . . confusion, obscurity are part of knowledge; noise is part of communication, part of the house."[25]

Diderot himself must have sensed that he had created a paradigm-breaking narrative, because, as Herbert Dieckmann notes, "he hesitates among several terms to define the genre of *La Religieuse*. In the *Préface*, he uses the terms 'letter,' 'memoirs,' 'story,' 'narrative,' 'novel,' 'satire.' "[26] But this transformation of narrative models has implications that go beyond the question of the evolution of genres. Diderot is operating within a perspective that implies the rejection of reversible narrative models on the basis of their insufficiency to represent the "real" and, in this specific instance, of their inability to account for the complexity of a person's experience of "real" time. In his search for a model of the complexity of the experience of time—one that, as I shall argue in Chapter 4, would serve as a model for human history—Diderot associates and combines on a trial basis various components of what I shall henceforth call "complex narrative time." Fiction offers the experimental terrain for Diderot to try out his model of narrative time and therefore his definition of history. This in turn explains why Diderot's fiction has always been considered the most conceptually fertile part of his oeuvre. Though critics have always sensed the importance of Diderot's fiction to his philosophy, they have not always spelled out the reasons for this. We will begin to get an idea of the reasons if we turn to a text that explicitly addresses the question of history: the *Essai sur les règnes de Claude et de Néron*.

CHAPTER FOUR

DETOURS THROUGH TIME AND SPACE

DIDEROT'S LATE HISTORICAL WRITINGS

Happy is the systematic philosopher to whom nature has given, as it did long ago to Epicurus, Lucretius, Aristotle, and Plato, a strong imagination, great eloquence, the art of presenting his ideas by means of striking and sublime images! The edifice that he has constructed can one day fall down; but his statue will remain standing in the middle of its ruins; and the rock that will break loose from the mountain will not destroy it, because the statue's feet are not made out of clay.

— Diderot, *Pensées sur l'interprétation de la nature*

The problems of narrative and narrative temporality, so important in Diderot's fiction, particularly in *La Religieuse*, take on a greater urgency in his historical writings. Historical discourse, after all, depends on the historian's ability to establish a homology between the temporal pattern of events and the narrative pattern in which he or she recounts them.[1] In his late historical writings, Diderot again puts the narrative model from *La Religieuse* to the test. And predictably, as we now can imagine from having studied the deviations from narrative and temporal norms in *La Religieuse*, Diderot's efforts yield a text that bears little resemblance to traditional historical accounts. This is certainly the case with the *Essai sur les règnes de Claude et de Néron*, the last complete work Diderot wrote and published. It is a work that has come under critical fire for what J. Robert Loy has called its lack of historical rigor and its "loose and incoherent form."[2] A different picture of the *Essai* emerges, however, if we take into account Diderot's experiences as a collaborator on the Abbé Raynal's *Histoire des Deux Indes*. These experiences, as we shall see, were decisive in shaping the approach to history and historical narrative that Diderot was subsequently to adopt in the *Essai sur les règnes de Claude et de Néron*.

THE "HISTOIRE DES DEUX INDES"

If I were allowed to venture a prediction, I would announce that very soon thinking minds will turn to the study of history, that immense quarry in which philosophy has not yet set foot.

— From a passage by Diderot for the *Histoire des Deux Indes*

When Diderot wrote the preceding passage, he was not so much predicting that philosophy would soon focus its attention on history, which, according to him, philosophy had so far left untouched, as describing the very endeavor in which he himself was currently engaged. He had recently been enlisted by the Abbé Raynal to collaborate on a historical account of the European colonization of the East and West Indies, to be entitled *Histoire philosophique et politique des établissements et du commerce des Européens dans les deux Indes* (Philosophical and political history of European settlements and commerce in the two Indies).[3]

Though the European colonization had been studied extensively and had already inspired a number of moral, civil, political, and natural histories, none had as yet been written that examined the problem from both a political and a philosophical perspective. As such, the Abbé Raynal's *Histoire des Deux Indes* purported to provide not just an account of European commerce and colonization in the East Indies and in the Americas, but also a philosophy of history. The *Histoire* was therefore innovative not just because of the unusual approach it took to an important subject but also because of the magnitude of its scope: "For the natural, moral, civil, and political histories of the colonies such as they were written up to that point, Raynal substitutes a vast fresco, a global history, one might say, which breaks away from the existing 'divisions' and laws of historical discourse."[4] A project of such vast proportions, however, proved beyond Raynal's capacities, and as a result he enlisted Diderot to compose the passages that would give the *Histoire des Deux Indes* the philosophical dimension that Raynal deemed essential to it. More specifically, Diderot's task was to speculate both on the notion of history and on the impact that the process of colonization had had on it. For himself Raynal reserved the task of weaving the principal events of the European colonization into a coherent narrative.

This division of labor meant that Raynal's and Diderot's respective assignments bore little relation to each other. Each *philosophe* faced a different set of problems concerning both form and content for which he had to find some solution. Raynal's was the more traditionally historical task; Diderot's was the more philosophical. The narrative structures that each derived therefore embody the difference in their approaches. This makes the *Histoire des Deux Indes* a particularly suitable place to examine the differences between the assumptions implicit in traditional historical writing and those that inform the idiosyncratic approach that Diderot began to forge in the *Histoire*.

It is not surprising to find that Raynal chose to recount the events in the colonization of the East and West Indies in chronological order, since this was the standing convention for historical writing. Thus, for example, in the section of the *Histoire* that examines Dutch colonization, Raynal surveys in chronological order both the principal events in the history of Holland and the principal events in that nation's efforts to establish colonies, beginning with the first Dutch voyages to the Indies and continuing with later attempts to found colonies in Formosa and other distant lands.[5]

The structure of traditional historical narrative assumes that the relationship between the various events in the life of a civilization become readable into the distant past or future once those events are arranged within the temporal continuum known as chronological order. It is possible to make this assumption, however, only if one also assumes that events in history are linked in a continuous cause-and-effect relation and that chronological narrative structure reproduces that relation. What supposedly guarantees the reliability of this particular brand of history, in other words, is the homology that it purports to establish between the order of events—whether in nature, politics, or society—and the structure of the narrative in which those events are described.

That Raynal was operating under these assumptions is evident in the following passage from the *Histoire des Deux Indes*:

> Before we follow [the Dutch] to these vast regions [the seas and land masses of the two Indies], we shall go back in time to the most ancient epoch in [Holland's] history. It is especially fitting in a work of this particular nature to embrace with a rapid glance everything that can characterize the spirit of a nation. It is necessary to place within reach of the thinking reader the possibility of judging whether or not what [Holland] was at its origins heralded what it has become since then; and if the worthy companions of Civilis, who braved the Roman powers, continue to exist in those intrepid republicans who, under the auspices of Nassau, beat back the dark and hateful tyranny of Philip II.[6]

The answers that Raynal will subsequently give to the rhetorical questions he poses in the preceding passage imply that he does indeed see events in the Dutch past as the determining causes of the Dutch present, a conclusion that becomes inescapable once those events are arranged chronologically. In the end, then, although Raynal broke with tradition when he decided on the subject and scope of the *Histoire des Deux Indes*, he followed the traditional historical model when he drafted his own contributions to it.

Diderot, on the other hand, took an altogether different course. From the very beginning, he had to grapple with a double problem of form. The first problem arose because Raynal had already written a substantial portion of the narrative of the *Histoire* by the time he asked Diderot to collaborate. Diderot therefore initially had to resort to drafting his own contributions in the form of fragments that could be intercalated within Raynal's text. To allow for the inclusion of his own passages within the larger whole, Diderot then found that he had to revise Raynal's narrative in detail. As a result, by the time Diderot stopped working on the *Histoire*, he not only had drafted an extensive set of his own passages but had also essentially revised the entire second edition of the *Histoire* and rewritten most of the third.[7]

Although on the one hand Diderot did not have much choice as to the form of his contributions, on the other hand the unusual nature of his assignment freed him from a different set of constraints. Because he did not have to concern himself with retelling historical events, but instead had to supply philosophical reflections, isolated meditations, Diderot did not have to follow chronological order. This was the source of a second decision to be made concerning appropriate format. In fact, chronology proved to be so irrelevant to the import of his contributions that when the passages he wrote for the *Histoire* were prepared for publication as a separate text, they were grouped not according to any temporal pattern but according to theme.[8]

Diderot's purpose in the *Histoire* was not conducive to the production of a text resembling traditional historical narrative. So although Diderot's original intention had been to weave his fragments seamlessly into Raynal's narrative, the difference in the tone and content of each *philosophe*'s writings was such that their individual voices could still be heard, despite Diderot's efforts to blend them into one. In the end, Diderot's metahistorical passages provided a counterpoint to Raynal's, a commentary, and hence disrupted the narrative continuity characteristic of traditional historical narratives. As a result, the

Histoire became a text that conveyed more than just a mere understanding of particular historical events. Because the philosophical interpolations fragment the chronology and the chronology interferes with the philosophical commentary, the reader can never be entirely absorbed into one mode or the other. The *Histoire des Deux Indes* is therefore a text that cannot be fully assimilated to what had become more or less the contemporary convention for historical discourse, that is, the kind of presentation used by Voltaire in *Le Siècle de Louis XIV*.

The reader of the *Histoire des Deux Indes* is forced to reflect constantly, to reevaluate constantly the weight of any particular event or conclusion, not only with respect to the other events or conclusions, but also, perhaps even primarily, with respect to his own understanding of the function of historical writing. Diderot's contributions to the *Histoire*, in other words, pull the reader out of the context of traditional history. Rather than passively absorbing the information being transmitted, the reader is, through interruption of the flow by these philosophical meditations, somewhat akin to the procedure used in *Jacques*, maneuvered into a new vantage point with respect to the historical events and the act of history writing itself. He is forced into the role of a metahistorian.

So far we have concentrated on the circumstances of collaboration that led Diderot to deviate from the norms of historical writing. There are other reasons, however, reasons intrinsic to Diderot's own evolving conception of history, that also contributed to these deviations. It is impossible to understand Diderot's conception of history without realizing that it is inextricably tied to his idiosyncratic view of the working of nature.

According to the then dominant Newtonian view, nature's functional principle is the law of cause and effect, which holds that once an event in nature has been observed, it is possible not only to deduce the cause of that event but also to predict its long-term consequences. This model is based on the definition of nature that underlay the notion of reversible narrative discussed in the last chapter: the assumption that the fundamental law of continuous cause and effect is unchanging and remains stable over time. In Diderot's universe, quite to the contrary, the laws of nature are not stable. As he had earlier claimed in the *Pensées sur l'interprétation de la nature*, nature cannot be depended on to follow the law of cause and effect consistently, because the passage of time will quite literally change the laws of nature themselves. As a result, for Diderot the relation between events in time is not necessarily deterministic. He makes this point in the *Rêve de d'Alembert*: "The cause undergoes too many particular vicissitudes that escape us for us to count infallibly on the effect that will ensue."[9]

These views are echoed in some of the passages that Diderot drafted for the *Histoire des Deux Indes*. With one stroke, he eliminates the notion that nature functions according to the law of cause and effect: "Chance, which is the imperceptible current of nature, never rests and serves all men equally."[10] And he does not neglect to explore the implications of such a view for historical knowledge: "Men, and their knowledge and conjectures, whether focused on the past or on the future, are subject to the laws and movements of the whole of nature, which follows its own course, regardless of our projects and our thoughts, maybe even of our very existence, which, like nature, is nothing more than the momentary aftermath of a fleeting order."[11] Though historians—those who come up with "knowledge" and "conjectures" about the past and sometimes about the future—may attempt to impose causal models on the events they observe, those events are subject to the whim of nature, taking place at random and not according to any rules.[12] The Diderotian historian, therefore, unlike the classical historian, is in the position of the observer of nature, who must accept that his object of study is changing in ways that he cannot predict or perceive. As a result, historical knowledge can never be certain, nor can it provide a definitive view of the past, let alone a reliable way of predicting the future. The historian's difficulties are further compounded by the vantage point that he must adopt relative to the events he studies. In the *Histoire*, Diderot hints that the passage of time is another factor that erases the readability of events and therefore blocks the historian's comprehension of the past. Alluding to a developmental gap between the Americas and Europe, Diderot writes: "Who knows if in three or four thousand years, the current history of the Americas won't be as muddled, as inexplicable for its inhabitants, as the history of Europe prior to the Roman Republic is for us now?"[13] From the long-range perspective, the historian's understanding of the events of the past will be "muddled" and "inexplicable." Over a great enough period of time, because the laws of nature change, the reader who insists on occupying the vantage point used to understand reversible narrations can no longer be sure of reading, or even perhaps of perceiving, a cause-and-effect relation between events with any sureness.

But the question is not even this simple. One might assume that the way to avoid unreadability would be to limit historical analysis to events in the recent past. But here too there are problems.

> There is no doubt that a historian who dares to write about the events of his own century rarely has any reliable insights. The councils of kings are a sanctuary whose curtain is only lifted with a slow hand by time. Their ministers, whether maintaining the cover of secrecy out of loyalty or because they have something to gain from doing so, speak only in order to mislead in its investigations the curiosity of whoever attempts to penetrate those secrets. No matter how much shrewdness he may employ to uncover the origin of events and the links between them, he will be reduced to guessing. Even when he attains his goal, he only does so without realizing it, or without daring to assert it; this uncertainty is scarcely more satisfying than total ignorance.

... These considerations ought to stop whoever is interested only in following the thread of political intrigues. He himself falls apart at the same time that they are being formed.[14]

Those who try to write from the vantage point of the present or who look back on the recent past are forced to guess what the causes and links of political events may be, since it is only with the passing of time—"[the] curtain is only lifted with a slow hand by time"—that they become visible. Though this claim may at first appear to contradict Diderot's contention that time *erases* the readability of events, he in fact is drawing a distinction between events in human history and events in natural history. Unlike the latter, events in human history have to do with reactions and motivations and therefore the very human action of hiding them constitutes in itself a historical event. In this instance, time unveils what humans hide, by making private memoirs available after their authors die and can no longer be at risk for revealing state secrets. More specifically, then, Diderot's claim is that political history cannot be written from the vantage point of the contemporary observer. The events are not available to contemporary observation. They can therefore be written about only from a retrospective vantage point. The attempt to salvage the vantage point of reversible narration is therefore doomed by the peculiar nature of human historical events.

But just because the historian cannot talk about cause-and-effect relationships between events directly does not mean that he has no other way to gain access to contemporary history. The substance of this history lies instead in the personal details that underlie and bring about the events themselves.

> If it is wise at this point to remain silent about the obscure causes of events, it is the appropriate time to speak about the character traits of the actors. We know what they were like during childhood, in youth, in maturity, what they were like within the family and in society; in private life and in business; what their nat-

ural aptitudes were, their acquired talents, their dominant passions, their vices, their virtues. . . . It is into the soul of one of the most important personages of the century that we seek to penetrate, and this is perhaps the most propitious moment for doing so. Posterity, which receives little more than bold outlines, will be deprived of the thousands of simple and innocent details that enlighten the contemporary observer.[15]

Here Diderot seems to be calling for biographies written from the perspective of the contemporary observer. The importance of this historical genre should not be underestimated, for it is the personal characteristics and private actions of politicians, which a contemporary observer is in the best position to analyze, that are frequently the prime movers of history: "an amusing remark . . . a frivolous whim . . . a small resentment . . . a puerile outburst of jealousy: for those are the marvelous levers with which we have so often turned the world upside down, and with which it shall no doubt often be turned upside down again."[16]

For Diderot, then, there exists no one vantage point that allows the historian to come up with a complete picture of the cause-and-effect interrelations of historical events. From whatever perspective he may view events in the past or present, he will always come upon lacunae and obscurities. As a result, reversible historical narratives will always be plagued by uncertainty and ambiguity.

Diderot's critique of the traditional historian's vantage point also leads to an apparent contradiction. Although it is never possible to eliminate all the uncertainty and ambiguity inherent in whatever perspective the historian adopts, uncertainty and ambiguity will be minimized if political history is written as if it were biography and if biography is written as if it were political history. Or, to put it another way, the historian must write the history of contemporary times as if he were writing about the past and the history of the distant past as if he were writing about contemporary times.

Can this contradiction be resolved, or at least made to function as historical discourse? It is my view that Diderot was grappling with this question when he wrote the *Essai sur les règnes de Claude et de Néron*.

THE "ESSAI SUR LES RÈGNES DE CLAUDE ET DE NÉRON"

Although Diderot's contributions to the *Histoire* remained anchored to Raynal's narrative framework, his subsequent historical production suggests that the formal strictures imposed by his collaboration with Raynal left their mark on his conception of historical discourse. There is evidence for this claim in Diderot's plans to publish his contributions to the *Histoire des Deux Indes* as a series of separate fragments. The *Essai sur les règnes de Claude et de Néron* presents a particularly interesting attempt on Diderot's part to develop the fragmentary writing that characterized his first sustained encounter with the historical genre.

The *Essai sur les règnes de Claude et de Néron* is a two-part historical work, the first of which recounts the life of Seneca as well as the principal political events of the reigns of Claudius and Nero. The first part is therefore less unconventional as a historical narrative than the second, which consists of an extensive critical commentary on Seneca's writings. But even the first part of the *Essai*, the more properly historical of the two, is characterized by unexpected and seemingly illogical digressions and jumps in chronology. Diderot, moreover, frequently abandons the conventional narrative voice of historical accounts — the third person — for the more personal and literary first person. And he often intersperses his narrative, whether in the first or third person, with imaginary dialogues between historical figures. These departures from historical convention, however, follow a logic derived from Diderot's experiences as a collaborator on the *Histoire des Deux Indes*.

Diderot's research on the history of colonization, as we saw earlier, had led him to propose unusual kinds of narrative temporality in which the past is encoded as the present and the present as the past. This preoccupation with the relationship between the present and past both in real life and in narration resurfaces in the *Essai*. Here Diderot extends the problem beyond the questions of effective narration to speculations about relations between past and present events. He draws the reader's attention to the analogies between the reigns of Claudius and Nero and his own eighteenth-century France. Commenting on a text written by Seneca, for example, Diderot observes:

> The similarity between our customs and those of [Seneca's] time is sometimes so remarkable that you go from the translation back to the original to assure yourself of them. "I would like," [Seneca] says, "for Cato to meet one of our fashionable men, preceded by his heralds, his postilions, his black slaves, all enveloped in the same whirlwind of dust." . . . You would almost think that you are on the road to Versailles.[17]

At other times the analogy between the two historical periods remains implicit, as in the following description of the emperor Claudius:

> It is as if Claudius were stupefied . . . sometimes he forgets who he is . . . where he is, in which place, at which moment, to whom he is speaking; he invites to supper citizens whom he had put to death the previous day; at table he asks a guest why he has come without his wife, when this wife had died; after Messalina's death, he complains that the empress is taking too long to appear. (63)

As Jules Assézat informs us in a note to his 1875 edition of the *Essai sur les règnes de Claude et de Néron*, Louis XV had been known to act and speak in virtually the same manner.[18] The choice of historical setting for the *Essai* thus allows Diderot to embody in this text the kind of temporality he had speculated about in the *Histoire*, a temporality in which the past resonates with the present and the present with the past. The *Essai*'s setting also permits Diderot to circumvent some of the limitations that are characteristic of the vantage points available to the historian by allowing him (1) to adopt the retrospective vantage point that will enable him to "see" a panorama of historical events in the distant past and (2) to adopt simultaneously the vantage point of the contemporary observer that will permit him to "see" the seemingly insignificant daily actions of politicians, those actions whose role in history, as Diderot had remarked in the *Histoire*, cannot be underestimated.

But Diderot adds a further twist to the interaction between past and present in the *Essai* by drawing an analogy between himself and the historical figures about whom he writes. In the introduction, for instance, he tells the reader: "It will soon become clear that it is as much my soul that I am describing as that of the other characters who offer themselves up to my narrative" (36). The character with whom Diderot most closely identifies, however, is Seneca. He repeatedly points out the uncanny resemblances between himself and the Stoic philosopher. Having said about himself "I do not compose, I am not an author at all" (36), Diderot subsequently notes that Seneca "does not compose, he pours his mind and his soul out on paper" (258). In the second book of the *Essai*, furthermore, Diderot alludes to the similarities in their writing styles. And throughout the *Essai* he catalogues the numerous convergences between his own ideas and Seneca's.

There is even a moment in the *Essai* when the boundaries that separate Diderot's text from Seneca's seem to disappear. This happens at the beginning of the chapter in which he examines Seneca's ideas about happiness. As he does throughout the second part of the *Essai*, Diderot begins his commentary with a quotation that, as in previous instances, appears to have been taken from the ancient philosopher's writings: "There is no happiness without virtue" (343). Although this statement sums up Seneca's major thesis about happiness, it turns out not to be his. It is instead the concluding sentence of Diderot's *Essai sur le mérite et la vertu*. The transposition of Diderot's text into Seneca's creates a literal, instead of just a virtual, interpenetration between his thoughts and Seneca's, between Seneca's texts and his.

Yet even more important than Diderot's reminders about the resemblances between the form and content of Seneca's writings and his are the implicit allusions that he makes to the parallels in their two lives. As Jean Starobinski notes:

> Certain similarities jump out from the page, even though Diderot carefully avoided making explicit a comparison that would have been in bad taste. Seneca is a "provincial": Diderot is also. Seneca's father made "useless efforts to steer his son away from philosophy"; Diderot had also been subjected to the same paternal entreaties. Seneca had been exiled to Corsica; Diderot had been imprisoned at Vincennes, and doubtless it was not without having first made certain pledges to the established powers that each recovered his "freedom."[19]

Furthermore, Seneca's position as adviser to Nero mirrors Diderot's as political adviser to Catherine II of Russia, a position that made Diderot uncomfortable and which was one of the motivations for writing the *Essai*. This parallel has been discussed at length by critics of the *Essai*, who argue that Diderot's defense of Seneca's association with Nero is an indirect defense of his own relationship with Catherine, who, as Diderot eventually discovered to his great dismay, claimed to espouse his precepts on enlightened monarchy but instead systematically violated them.[20] In fact, so striking are the similarities between Seneca's life and Diderot's that in response to Seneca's remark that he has given too much of his time to others and therefore has not devoted enough time to his work, Diderot exclaims, "I didn't stop blushing as I read chapter 3; it is the story of my life" (371).

Indeed Diderot could claim that the whole of the *Essai* is "the story of [his] life." One can even speculate that Diderot, who unlike Rousseau never wrote a formal autobiography, meant the *Essai* to be read as one. There is no doubt, for example, that at the beginning of the *Essai* Diderot adopts the classic stance of the autobiographer. He is careful to note that he begins drafting this text at a point when he finds himself removed from the society of other people and, sensing that he is approaching the end of his life, decides to look back upon its principal events.

> This essay . . . is the product of . . . my leisure . . . during one of the most pleasant periods of my life. I was in the country, almost alone, free of cares and worries. . . . The years hadn't left behind any of those passions that have the power to torment, none of the boredom that usually follows them; I had lost my taste for the frivolities that we are led to hold in such great esteem because of our hope of enjoying them for a long time. Since I was nearing the end point at which everything vanishes, I aspired to nothing more than the approval of my own conscience and that of several friends. (35)

But Diderot speaks directly about himself only for the length of one paragraph. From this point on, in a significant move, he takes a detour through Seneca to tell his own story.

Why does Diderot go to such lengths to establish an almost supernatural affinity between himself and Seneca, to the point that writing about Seneca becomes the equivalent of writing about himself? We can begin to answer this question if we return for a moment to *La Religieuse*.

The identification that Diderot establishes between himself and Seneca in the *Essai* echoes a narrative strategy that he had earlier used successfully in *La Religieuse*. In this work Suzanne Simonin, the narrator, goes through a series of experiences that gradually cause her to lose her innocence. The knowledge that she gains through these experiences, furthermore, allows her to distinguish between her present (the time when she knows what she now knows) and her past (the time when she did not know what she now knows). But at the moment when she begins to recount her story, Suzanne suppresses the knowledge that she has acquired. By so doing, she ends up conflating the two temporal categories and turning her present into her past and her past into her present. Diderot's character thus forces his reader into an unusual and *non*judgmental relationship with respect to the events being recounted. The reader does not judge, he sympathizes.

In the *Essai*, the alleged identification with Seneca works in a similar way. The premise that Seneca is another Diderot and that Diderot is another Seneca allows Diderot to create the illusion that he and his alter ego have transcended temporal barriers, that the differences between past and present have melted away. This in turn allows Diderot to maintain the fiction that he is viewing the events that he recounts not retrospectively, like conventional historians, but as if he were an eyewitness. The narrative strategy that Diderot had earlier used in *La Religieuse* becomes a powerful historical tool in the *Essai*, a tool that allows him to create points of entry into the past for himself.

Though Diderot insists throughout the *Essai* on the many analogies that can be drawn between ancient Rome and France and between Seneca and himself, it would be a misrepresentation to claim that Diderot mentions only the similarities, for there are places in the *Essai* where he points to the divergences between them. In the introduction to the second part of the *Essai*, for example, Diderot mentions that he has some differences of opinion with Seneca that he will not conceal in his commentary on Seneca's principal works.

> I shall speak about Seneca's works impartially and without bias. Availing myself in my dealings with him of a privilege from which he never deviated with any other philosopher, I shall

sometimes dare to contradict him. . . . I shall therefore begin with the Letters . . . sometimes corroborating, and at other times refuting them; here, exposing to the censor the philosopher behind whom I keep myself hidden; there, playing the opposite role and offering myself as a target for arrows that will only wound Seneca, hidden behind me. (229)

True to this promise, Diderot does not hesitate to take issue with Seneca. For example, he quotes Seneca as saying that he likes to learn only in order to teach, and then proceeds to disagree with him: "I like to learn only so that I'll be less ignorant" (232). And again quoting Seneca, "The most beautiful discovery would cease to please me if it were only for my own benefit," Diderot continues: "Even if it were only for my own benefit, the simplest discovery would still please me. If chance presents me with a beautiful unknown page, I rejoice doubly in it, both for the admiration that it elicits in me and for the hope of showing it to my friends" (232).

One reason why Diderot remarks not just on the similarities but also on the differences between ancient Rome and contemporary France, and between himself and Seneca, is that he is working with a notion of time and history that takes change into account. Yet in demonstrating the remarkable similarities between the two historical periods and the two philosophers, Diderot shows that he is also working with a notion of time that produces repetitions of the past in the present. His point is that within the global variances produced by the passage of time there nevertheless can be local instances of invariance. He formulates this idea explicitly when he begins to describe his relationship with Seneca. Addressing himself to his designated alter ego, Diderot says: "What am I to you? and what bond, *spared by time*, can possibly subsist between us?" (39, my emphasis). The claim that there exists a link between Diderot and Seneca that has been spared by time implies, on the one hand, that time is an agent of change that would normally make the subsistence of such a link impossible. On the other hand, his claim that the link does indeed subsist implies what looks like a local reversal of time that has created a theoretically impossible relationship.

This "reversal" of time takes place not because Diderot manages literally to make events move backwards in time, but rather as a result of his experience of reading. It is through the careful reading and rereading of Tacitus's and Suetonius's accounts of Seneca, as well as the careful reading and rereading of Seneca's own works, that Diderot has gained an intimate, almost physical, familiarity with him, just like the familiarity that the reader of Suzanne Simonin's memoirs or the reader of a statesman's private papers develops. For Diderot, the act of reading recreates the experience of being with Seneca, of seeing him as he goes through his daily life, of having him as a friend. Indeed it is as if Seneca were brought back to life by the act of reading, just as the nun is. As we shall now see, this is exactly the experience that he then attempts to recreate for the reader of the *Essai*. To do this, he calls on his findings about historical narrative from the *Histoire des Deux Indes*.

Diderot's position as collaborator on the *Histoire des Deux Indes* required that he draft his contributions in the form of fragments, fragments that were subsequently inserted into the framework of Raynal's narrative. Diderot, moreover, spent long hours smoothing over any rough seams produced by the interweaving of the two texts. The result is a work possessing both structural and thematic complexity, and yet the difference in subject and tone between the two authors' contributions make the *Histoire* a work in which two distinct voices can still be heard.

These features of Diderot's contributions to the *Histoire* resurface in the *Essai sur les règnes de Claude et de Néron*. It too consists of a series of fragments—two main sections, each of which in turn is broken up into books and then into subsections numbered with Roman numerals. Diderot himself alludes to the fragmentary form of the *Essai* in the introduction to the first book, in which he compares one of the ways in which it is possible to read the *Essai* to the way one would read texts by La Rochefoucauld or La Bruyère (36). But Diderot is also careful to state that, unlike La Rochefoucauld's maxims or La Bruyère's chapters, the *Essai*'s fragments are not discrete entities. Although physically dissociated from the texts of Suetonius, Tacitus, and Seneca, the *Essai*'s fragments are nevertheless intricately bound to them, as Diderot insists in the introduction to the first book of the *Essai*. In other words, fragmentation by itself is not enough.

And in much the same way that he had inserted his contributions to the *Histoire des Deux Indes* in the interstices of Raynal's narrative, Diderot claims that he has written his biography of Seneca (the first book of the *Essai*) "in the margins" of texts already drafted by others, in this instance Tacitus, Suetonius, and Seneca himself. Where the *Histoire* incorporated two authorial voices, however, the *Essai* augments the polyphony, giving voice not just to Diderot and Seneca but also to two other authors from the ancient world.[21] In a passage that sounds like an Enlightenment update of Montaigne, he says:

> An experiment that I would gladly propose to a man age sixty-five or sixty-six, who might judge [my reflections] to be either too long or too numerous, or too foreign to the subject, is to go off alone taking Tacitus, Suetonius, and Seneca with him; to jot down casually on paper the things that interest him, the ideas that they evoke in his mind, the thoughts of the various authors that he would like to retain, the feelings that he might experience, having no other design than to educate himself without exhausting himself: and I am almost certain that if he were to stop in the same places where I stopped, if he were to compare his era to past eras, and if on the basis of particular features and circumstances he were to make the same conjectures on what the pres-

ent augurs, on what we can expect or fear from the future, he would recreate this work almost exactly as it is now. (36)

Two points need to be dealt with here: (1) the nature of the polyphonic text and (2) the issue of the reproducibility of the message. First, the issue of the polyphonic text. Diderot's claim that his own discourse is evolving on the borders of texts written by others applies not just to the first book of the *Essai* but to the entire work. At the beginning of the *Essai*'s second part, which, as mentioned earlier, consists of an extensive commentary on Seneca's writings, Diderot again claims to be writing in the margins of someone else's texts— this time Seneca's alone: "I shall therefore begin [my analysis of Seneca's works] with the Letters, transporting what he says in one letter to another, generalizing his maxims, and restricting them, commenting on them, and applying them in my own fashion" (229). It is through the implicit interplay in the second half of the *Essai* between Seneca's works and Diderot's commentary, and in the first half between Tacitus's and Suetonius's accounts of Seneca and his own, that Diderot attempts to reproduce the polyphonic quality of the *Histoire*.

In this chorus from the distant past, however, one voice predominates: Seneca's. Diderot virtually grants him the status of coauthor when he tells the reader that if he wants to understand the *Essai*, he must glance back and forth between Seneca's text and Diderot's.

> If [the reader of the *Essai*] hears only my voice, he will reproach me for being incoherent, perhaps even obscure, especially in those places where I examine Seneca's works; and he will read me, though not necessarily with as much pleasure, in the same way one reads the *Maximes* of La Rochefoucauld and a chapter of La Bruyère. But if the reader casts his eyes alternately on a page of Seneca and on one of mine, he will notice more order, more clarity, in the latter, insofar as he will put himself faithfully in my place, as he will find a greater or lesser degree of analogy between

himself and the philosopher, between himself and me; and he will soon realize that it is as much my own soul I am portraying as that of the different personages who offer themselves up to my narrative. (36)

The portion of the preceding passage cited earlier establishes the *Essai* as consisting of a series of fragments. But the rest of the passage suggests that Diderot imagines his fragmented comments as existing not in isolation but rather in tandem with Seneca's writings. This notion of the *Essai* as a text that incorporates two authorial voices harks back to the *Histoire* and the resonances in it of both Diderot's and Raynal's authorial voices. But there is nevertheless an important difference here. In the *Histoire* Diderot had woven his fragments into Raynal's text to create as continuous a narrative as he could. But in the *Essai* Diderot's fragments and Seneca's works remain textually discontinuous (which serves at one level to remind the reader *at first glance* that Diderot is writing not about Seneca as a historical subject but along with Seneca). The question now is why Diderot chose to reverse the procedure he had followed in the *Histoire* by dissociating his fragments from Seneca's texts, which he nevertheless imagines as their intertext.

The answer to this question should be obvious by now. The radical discontinuity between the texts Diderot himself defines as being the two essential components of the *Essai* fulfills a typically Diderotian strategy: it is designed to engage the reader actively in the generation of the narrative of the *Essai*. In the passage quoted above, Diderot states explicitly that it is the *reader* who must create the dynamic textual interplay that Diderot seeks to establish between his own work and Seneca's. Indeed he instructs the reader not to read the *Essai* by itself but rather to cast "his eyes alternately on a page of Seneca and on one of mine" (36). This back-and-forth reading pattern reproduces the process Diderot himself underwent when reading Seneca and the works of Tacitus and Suetonius.

Implicit in Diderot's assignation of this novel position to the reader of historical accounts is a unique conception of historical discourse. In the *Essai*, Diderot seems merely to be presenting the reader with materials from Seneca, Tacitus, and Suetonius, along with his own commentary of these texts. But now it is up to the reader, and no longer to Diderot, to make the necessary links between these textual fragments. What the *Essai* emphasizes is not the content of history as the description of events in the past but the operations involved in constructing a description of those events. By fragmenting his text and refusing to give it a fixed narrative framework, Diderot forces the reader to do the work of a historian, or in other words, to experience the historian's process of becoming familiar with the past. For Diderot, then, the past is a construct that the reader actively creates in his mind and historical discourse is the process that allows him to actively experience the construction of an understanding of the past. Whereas what was most important about the *Histoire* was its content—the information about past events being transmitted to the reader—what is most important about the *Essai* is the process involved in the reconstruction of those events.

It should be clear at this point that the mechanism Diderot is using to force the reader to actively reproduce the work of a historian provides yet another instance of the *Préface-annexe*'s open ternary model of communication. That this is indeed the case is evident in the various conversational exchanges that he sprinkles throughout the *Essai*. Let us look for a moment at a dialogue between Seneca and Diderot on the subject of Seneca's *Apocolocyntosis*, a virulent satire of Claudius.

> [DIDEROT] What, O philosopher, you worship the sovereign basely during his lifetime and you insult him cruelly after his death!
> [SENECA] He couldn't do me any more harm.

[DIDEROT] That is the answer of a coward and an ingrate, for if he'd been your benefactor, you would have kept silent, since he couldn't do you any more good.
[SENECA] But he thought that I was guilty of adultery with Julia.
[DIDEROT] And what did it matter to you, if you weren't?
[SENECA] He kept me in exile for eight years. (385)

Diderot's recreation of this dispute with Seneca creates the illusion that he has left his own historical context and is therefore able to speak to Seneca face-to-face, as if Seneca were his contemporary. It is through conversations such as this one that Diderot can seemingly travel through time.

But Diderot holds dialogues not just with Seneca but also with the reader. In these exchanges, Diderot frequently formulates the reader's presumed agreements or disagreements with his own theses about Seneca. This is what he does, for example, in the following exchange between the "reader" and Diderot, on the subject of Seneca:

[READER] Seneca therefore has no defects?
[DIDEROT] He does, and I thought I'd pointed some of them out. (264)

At another point, the "reader" reminds Diderot that he has strayed from his subject:

[READER] But what about Seneca's letters? . . .
[DIDEROT] I'll come back to them when I can. I linger wherever I am at ease. (268)

In this instance, Diderot makes explicit a hypostatized reader's responses to his text, a technique that he had earlier used in *Jacques le fataliste*. These dialogues again allow Diderot to create the impression that he has traveled through time, except that this time he no longer goes back to the Rome of Claudius and Nero but instead moves toward the future, and specifically toward the reader's present, with whom he is now able to converse.

Diderot, furthermore, makes explicit allusions to his movements through time, as he turns the clock back to describe the events in the Rome of Claudius and Nero as if he were an eyewitness and then jumps forward again in time to reenter his own temporal context. For instance, after a long passage about Rousseau, Diderot marks the shift from his own temporal context to that of ancient Rome by saying: "I return to Rome, and continue the diary of *my readings*" (131). Similarly, after recounting the death of Nero, he begins to speak as if he had moved back in time and were looking at Nero's cadaver: "I stand immobile before his cadaver. Every time I remember one of his crimes, I feel my indignation redouble; but what does it matter to him? he does not see me. It is in vain that I reproach him for the murders of Agrippina, Burrus, Seneca, Thrasea, Vetus and his family; he no longer hears me" (200).

But Diderot is not the only one whose promenades through time and space are facilitated by conversational exchanges, for he attempts to draw the reader into this process. In one instance, Diderot invites the reader to "listen in" on a hypothetical conversation that might have taken place among a group of Romans, had Seneca and Burrus decided to assassinate Nero: "Indeed let us sketch out popular hearsay about this assassination, had it taken place."

> [THE FIRST ROMAN] *They have killed him, as their own security and our sufferings counseled them to do.*
> [THE SECOND ROMAN] About whom are you speaking?
> [THE FIRST ROMAN] *I am speaking about Seneca, Burrus and Nero.* (137)

At another point, Diderot urges the reader to participate in his "interrogation" of Seneca: "Let us interrogate the philosopher before judging him: Seneca, what have you done with Nero?"

(95). Yet another exhortation to the reader to "enter" the past appears at a later point: "But let us join with the enemies of the wealthy philosopher, and let us interrogate him on the use of his riches" (181). Implicit in the first-person plural imperatives "let us sketch out," "let us interrogate," and "let us join with" is the inclusion of the reader in the exchanges.[22]

Diderot's and his reader's zigzags through time force them to abandon the vantage point of the conventional retrospective narrator and reader, who look back on the past from a stable point in the present and instead adopt an unstable vantage point that moves back and forth between different time periods. Diderot's strategy here is reminiscent of Suzanne Simonin's unusual brand of retrospective narration, whose consequences we saw in Chapter 3. Here, however, there initially seems to be no way to predict when one of these shifts will take place, since Diderot's movement from one temporal context to the other does not follow any logical, predictable pattern. Instead it seems to occur as if by chance, when something in the present evokes for him something in the past, and vice versa.

But these shifts serve several typically Diderotian purposes. The random shifts from one temporal context to another disrupt chronology and thus make the point that events in the past and in the present do not necessarily relate to one another in a deterministic fashion. This in turn allows Diderot to dissociate the question of temporality from the question of the relationship of events in the past to each other and place it instead in the context of the relationship between events that the reader perceives and experiences while he is reading the text.

Diderot's random shifts also undermine the reader's ability to predict where the narrative will take him next. By destabilizing the reader's position in this way, Diderot prevents him from acceding to the stable vantage point on the past that Diderot himself had earlier abandoned. This in turn prevents the reader from reconstituting the chronological order of the events he reads about in the *Essai*. The nonchronological logic of the *Essai*, which works by association (Diderot slips from one context to another when an event or person in one evokes for him the memory of an event or person in the other), allows Diderot to refrain from presenting the reader with predetermined conclusions about past events. It allows him, in other words, to avoid setting up cause-and-effect relationships between past and present; instead it sets up connotative resonances between them. Thus the temporal shifts in the *Essai* place the reader in a position where he will have to evaluate the material presented to him and draw his own conclusions, thereby forcing him to actively produce for himself a coherent account of the past. Ultimately, then, the random temporal shifts in the *Essai* make the reader do the work of a Diderotian metahistorian, just as in the *Histoire*.

By now it should be no surprise that ternary circuits again play a crucial role in engaging the active participation of the reader. As noted earlier, the *Essai* provides an additional instance of the open ternary model of communication we first discovered in the *Préface-annexe*. Now we can make this observation more precise, for as the textual examples from the preceding section reveal, the three terms bound within the transtemporal circuit of communication in the *Essai* are Diderot, Seneca, and the reader. However, their positions in the circuit are not stable. Each shift produces a variation on the ternary model using the same three components but privileges the relationships among them differently.

Diderot implicitly describes the first of these variations in the introduction to the first book of the *Essai*.

> I had a . . . worthy goal: to examine impartially the life and works of Seneca and to avenge a great man, if he'd been slandered; or, if I thought him guilty, to lament his weaknesses and profit from his wise and powerful lessons. Such was the frame of

mind in which I was writing, and such is the frame of mind in which I would hope to be read. (35)

All three terms in the communicational model make an appearance in this passage: Diderot in his role as historian, Seneca in his role as the subject of Diderot's history, and the reader as judge. In addition, Diderot defines the interrelationships of the three terms within the communicational circuit. He suggests that the *Essai*, if read in the proper spirit, will put the reader in touch with an important aspect of the European past, namely, the life and thought of Seneca. But the reader's access to that past will not be direct. For Diderot also makes it clear that he is interposing himself—as a third term—between the reader and Seneca, since his goal in writing the *Essai* is not just to analyze the life and works of Seneca impartially but also to exercise his judgment on other historians' accounts of him. Thus Diderot's purpose is also to "avenge a great man, if he'd been slandered; or, if I thought him guilty, to lament his weaknesses" (35). Diderot, in other words, is creating an interpretive filter through which he wants the reader to look at Seneca.

Specifically, he wants to change the negative view his contemporaries have of Seneca. According to Diderot, Seneca has been maligned through the centuries, as historians have claimed that he in fact encouraged and approved Nero's excesses. To this end, he puts into question the knowledge and judgment of those who have cast aspersions on Seneca. For instance, he calls the comments made about Seneca by Suillius, one of Seneca's contemporaries, "the impudent calumnies of a Suillius, the most contemptible man of his time" (65). Furthermore, after quoting Suillius's accusations and showing that they are unfounded, Diderot adds:

> It is the preceding speech that the Cassius Dios, the Xiphilinuses, and a swarm of other detractors of Seneca have continued to paraphrase, from Seneca's own time up to ours. It seems to me

that in order to rely on the imputations of a Suillius, an informer by profession, a madman, who has been sullied by, accused of, and punished for a thousand heinous crimes, one must be the victim of a cruel aversion to believing the opinions of upstanding men. (116–17)

Diderot thus establishes that Seneca's bad reputation, maintained by historians and commentators throughout the ages, is based largely on the accusations of a man whose opinion should not be trusted. In so doing, Diderot hopes to erase that interpretation of Seneca's actions and to be able to show him instead in a positive light, as a minister who fully disapproved of the actions Nero took in the latter part of his reign but who nevertheless was unable to stop him.

Returning to the question of the ternary communicational model, we can see that Diderot's description of this first relationship that obtains among historian, reader, and the past is fully conventional. Implicit in this relationship are the traditional assumptions about why one reads history (to see and understand the past), about what history is (an interpretation of events in the past), and about the way a reader of historical accounts is able to see the past (through the interpretive filter that Diderot, the historian, has constructed). Another assumption implicit in this relationship of reader, historian, and the past is that each entity has a particular temporal relation to the others. The historian is temporally distanced from the subjects he writes about (the historian inhabits a "present," and his subjects a "past"). The reader is also temporally distanced from the people and events in the account he reads and indeed even from the historian.

Up to this point there seem to be no serious differences between the model of history writing Diderot has sketched out and the traditional historical model. And because it is the first one he proposes in the *Essai*, we could assume that he will maintain it throughout. Very shortly thereafter, however, we discover another ternary circuit in the additional instructions Diderot gives to the reader.

In these instructions, Diderot urges the reader to approach the *Essai* in a curious way. Rather than reading the *Essai* by itself, the reader should instead read it in conjunction with Seneca's writings. The reader's task, as Diderot explicitly formulates it, is not just to read Diderot's account as a replacement for Seneca's own account but to construct a collage of Diderot's and Seneca's texts. Failing this, the *Essai* will be nothing more than noise for the reader: "If [the reader of the *Essai*] hears only my voice, he will reproach me for being incoherent, perhaps even obscure, especially in those places where I examine Seneca's works" (36). A direct exchange between Diderot ("my voice") and the reader will result in the reader's seeing Diderot's text as "incoherent" and "obscure." If, on the other hand, the reader actively introduces a third term—in this instance Seneca's texts—into the exchange, then the noise level in Diderot's *Essai* will be diminished: "But if the reader casts his eyes alternately on a page of Seneca and on one of mine, he will notice more order, more clarity, in the latter" (36). To gain access to Diderot and his ideas as represented in the *Essai*, then, the reader must take a detour through Seneca's writings.

In this variation of the ternary model, the operational terms are again Seneca, Diderot, and the reader. Seneca, however, serves only as a means to an end, as the factor that makes Diderot more comprehensible to the reader. This structure thus serves to place the emphasis not on Seneca but on Diderot. That it creates this displacement is significant, for Diderot's defense of Seneca's actions clearly springs from more than a mere desire to justify Seneca. The *Essai* is primarily an attempt to justify his own actions. The rehabilitation of Seneca that Diderot undertakes in the *Essai* thus also serves Diderot's own reputation, since it provides him with a mechanism to rehabilitate himself in the eyes of the reader, proving through Seneca that as an adviser one cannot dictate or control the actions of a head of state. But Diderot does not present his defense of Seneca in the form of a conventional argument, though it might have been easier and more effective to have done so. Instead he relies on the mechanism of the ternary communicational model to make his point. The question, of course, is why. We can begin to answer it by considering what Diderot's procedure accomplishes that a standard expository argument does not.

The first and most obvious answer to the question is that the ternary model as Diderot defines it in his instructions to the reader elicits the active participation of the reader. Rather than passively perusing an argument that has already been elaborated by someone else, the reader who follows Diderot's instructions is forced to interact both with Seneca's texts and with Diderot's.

What are the stakes of such a procedure? To begin with, it undermines the distance that separates both the traditional historian and the conventional reader from the objects of their scrutiny and also the distance that separates the conventional reader from the traditional historian, whose text is read not as a present but as the past. Traditional historical accounts assume that the past will remain a past, the present a present, and that no movement is possible between these static categories. Ternary circuits, on the other hand, establish different temporal relations. They work to abolish the distance between past and present, indeed to bring the past into the present. By insisting that the reader read both the *Essai* and Seneca at the same time, it is as if Diderot were situating all three terms of the circuit within the same time frame—and specifically the reader's own time frame. The process of reading seemingly pulls Seneca out of the distant past, pulls Diderot out of the recent past, and situates them instead within the reader's present. Had Diderot written a conventional defense of Seneca and even of himself, the temporal gap that separates both the historian and the reader from figures in the past and the historian from the reader would not have been bridged.

But why must this temporal gap be bridged in the first place? Diderot evidently wants to establish a unique relation between the historian and his object of study, and between the reader and the personages and events about which he reads. Specifically, Diderot wants to establish a more immediate relationship with Seneca, both for himself and for the reader. For in writing about Seneca, Diderot is not only writing about someone who lived in the past but also criticizing the work of another interpreter of Seneca, namely Suillius. And, as noted earlier, Diderot strenuously objects to the way that Suillius's interpretation of Seneca has taken the place of Seneca and of Seneca's texts and thereby continued to obscure them. His goal, therefore, is to bring Seneca out from under the cover of Suillius's interpretation. Nevertheless, because he writes a text like the *Essai*, Diderot could be accused of following the same procedure as Suillius, for if Diderot's attempted rehabilitation of Seneca succeeds, then his reading of Seneca will supersede Suillius's, still leaving Seneca himself hidden behind a new interpretive filter. In this case, Diderot's text would still be standing in for Seneca; Diderot would then merely be adopting the same position as the standard historian, whose accounts *become* the past for the reader. It is to prevent this from happening, to bring Seneca back out from the filters that obscure him, that Diderot pushes the reader to read Seneca for himself.

This is a point to which Diderot returns at several points in the *Essai*, not only in the introduction but also in the concluding sections of the *Essai*, where he makes a more passionate plea: "Read [Seneca], reread all his works, read Tacitus, and throw my apology into the fire, for it is only then that you will really be convinced that [Seneca] was a man of great talent and rare virtue, and that you will place his detractors in the most evil and unjust class of men" (399–400). In turn, Diderot needs to establish and maintain a dialogue with the reader *about* Seneca, as a way of reestablishing the immediacy of Diderot's own acquaintance with Seneca.

There is further evidence for this claim in Diderot's assigning the task of intertwining his and Seneca's texts to the reader. The reader in this instance functions as the third term to whom Diderot can talk and who thus makes it possible for him to interact with Seneca's text. It is a mechanism for making Seneca a functioning part of the philosophical and political present. Diderot, in other words, talks with Seneca through the reader as a way of drawing Seneca into the present.

In this particular instance of the ternary circuit, then, Diderot can trade places with Seneca, and Seneca with the reader. Whereas before we saw only Diderot interposed between the reader and Seneca, now we realize that it is just as valid to see Seneca interposed between the reader and Diderot, or the reader between Seneca and Diderot. The shift of function of the terms in the circuit determines who is communicating with whom, who is serving as intermediary.

That such shifts are possible brings into focus one of the unique features of Diderot's historical writing. Diderot's goal in writing history is not to show how the past made the present come about, for there is no direct cause-and-effect relation between the two, but rather to construct a model for seeing the present as though it were history. This represents a radical departure from the basic premise of traditional historical accounts. As we saw when we examined the *Histoire des Deux Indes*, one of the conventional assumptions of historical writing is that there has to be a temporal distance between the historian and the events about which he writes. Without this temporal distance, the historian will be unable to judge events, especially political events. But for Diderot what really matters in historical writing is not that the events being judged took place in the past, but that those events are being judged. For Diderot, in other words, history is an intellectual process—and not just a retelling of events that took place in the past—that allows one to judge the meaning of events. As a result, it can be applied not just to events in the past but also to events in the present.

With his ternary circuits, Diderot turns history into an interactive process of interpretation. Unlike more conventional notions of history, moreover, this interpretive process is the product not of observation of people, events, or texts but of interaction with those people, events, or texts. What Diderot's notion of history brings into sharper focus, then, is the present—recent or "contemporary" history—rather than the ancient past. (And at times the ancient past even becomes part of the historical present. We will return to this issue when we discuss Diderot's relationship to his friends.) The *Essai* is therefore meant not just to give the reader a view of the past through the eyes of an eighteenth-century *philosophe*, but also to give the reader a perspective on the eighteenth-century present and specifically of the intellectual perspective of the Enlightenment as Diderot defines it.

What is at stake here is the interpretation of political events. Diderot had stated in the *Histoire des Deux Indes* that the political can be talked about only in the past, because access to the information that would allow one to talk about it in the present is blocked. But one of the goals of Enlightenment philosophy is to find a way of talking about political events as they are occurring in the present and not just in the past, because the Enlightenment *philosophe engagé* must be able to judge events so that he can influence their course. The ternary circuits of the *Essai* fulfill that function, since they provide both the reader and the *philosophe* with the mechanism that allows them to interact with their political present.

This is clearly Diderot's response to the problem that Voltaire had posed succinctly in his article "Histoire" for the *Encyclopédie*.[23] Voltaire had observed, in much the same way as Diderot in the *Histoire des Deux Indes*, that it is possible to talk about political events only in the past, because in the present we cannot get access to the documents and the people that would allow us to talk about them in the present.[24] How is it possible to get around this problem? How is it possible to become politically active under these circumstances? For Enlightenment *philosophes* the answer to this question lies in a redefinition of the nature of history and the role of the historian. For them, history is not a process that consists merely of recounting past events but rather a process that allows one to discern the meaning of political events. The ideal Enlightenment history would therefore be a history of the present, and the ideal role of the historian would be to change the course of current events. What is at stake in this notion of history, in other words, is access to politics, specifically the possibility of engaging in political activity in the present.

Up to this point we have traced at least three shifts of the terms in the ternary model. These constantly occurring shifts are clearly strategically conceived, for they keep the reader off balance, never on any kind of sure footing. This in turn prevents the reader from resolving the model into an analytic structure, a structure that would allow him to gain mastery over its intellectual content. Diderot is trying instead to make the reader operate according to all three versions of the model at the same time. In other words, he is trying to force the reader at every moment into a mode that allows him to interact with the various models but does not allow him to bring them under his intellectual control by privileging one over another.

The constant interaction in which the reader is forced to engage, furthermore, is designed to prepare him for interaction of a more significant sort. Ultimately, it prepares him to become an active participant in the philosophical cabal. To understand how Diderot proposes to make the reader join the ranks of the philosophical cabal, however, we must take a closer look at a passage in which he recounts an experience from his own life.

> O Seneca, you are and will forever be, together with Socrates, all unfortunate illustrious men, and all the great men of antiquity, one of the most agreeable ties between my friends and me, between educated men of every generation and their friends. You have remained the subject of our frequent conversations, and you will remain the subject of theirs. (39)

Seneca has functioned in Diderot's experience as a third term in his relationship with his friends or, more specifically, as the subject of many conversations. The inclusion of Seneca in these exchanges has had two significant results. First, Seneca has been an important agent in creating affective bonds between Diderot and the people with whom he converses, as he implies by calling Seneca "one of the most agreeable ties between my friends and me." Second, Seneca has been instrumental in Diderot's ability to form not just personal bonds but also intellectual ones; any conversation whose principal subject is Seneca will perforce engage a discussion of his works and the ideas expressed in them. This is all the more likely since the participants (the friends to whom Diderot alludes in this passage) are other intellectuals, indeed other *philosophes*, as Diderot implies by juxtaposing the reference to "my friends and me" with a reference to "educated men of every generation." Finally, the claim that Seneca is and will continue to be "one of the most agreeable ties . . . between men of every generation and their friends" further suggests that Seneca's potential effectiveness in the creation of social and intellectual networks goes beyond the immediate circle of Diderot's fellow *philosophes* to encompass future generations of intellectuals.

The experience Diderot describes here is that of conversing in an eighteenth-century *salon*, where the interlocutors are *philosophes* and other enlightened intellectuals and where conversations have both an intellectual component (they are a verbal exchange of ideas) and a social one (they promote personal ties among the partisans of the Enlightenment—the group known as the philosophical cabal). Indeed Diderot identifies this process as constituting the object of philosophy: "What is the object of philosophy? To create links among men through an exchange of ideas, and through the practice of mutual acts of benevolence" (240).

The importance of Seneca in these philosophical discussions is twofold. First, Seneca's works and ideas provide a common ground that allows the interlocutors to begin to speak to each other. Second, because Seneca is a philosopher and because the interlocutors are discussing works in which he raises crucial philosophical issues, his inclusion as a "term" in the conversation helps the interlocutors to philosophize in turn. Their ability to do this is further facilitated by conversation itself, which is an open-ended form, and which, as a result of the process of response, interrogation, agreement, refutation, interruption, digression, and so forth that are characteristic of such exchanges, ultimately provides not a definitive content but rather a vehicle for encouraging potentially productive thought processes.[25]

This begins to explain why Diderot asks the reader to actively refer to Seneca's writings while he reads the *Essai*. His doing so allows Seneca to function as a third "interlocutor" in the exchange between the reader and Diderot, thereby recreating the structure of a typical *salon* conversation. But he does not always leave this process up to the reader. As we saw earlier, throughout the *Essai* he repeatedly includes the reader in "conversations" with Seneca and with other figures from the ancient Roman past.

We have now come full circle. Although the ternary model described above uses once again the same three terms (the reader, Diderot, and Seneca), their relationship has been turned upside down. Whereas what was at stake in the traditional and in the inverted historical models was the (future) *reader's* access to the past (Seneca) and the present (Diderot), what is at stake in this third instance is *Diderot's* access to the reader. Here Diderot tries to reproduce with the reader a strategy that had always been effective in generating intellectual activity among his friends. And it is precisely this kind of activity that he would like to encourage in the reader. Hence the importance of Diderot's use of conversational models in his writings. What is at stake in them is the possibility of transmitting something other than a content that the reader will absorb passively. Diderot's goal instead is to promote active thinking in the reader. Furthermore, Diderot's radical undermining of the traditional historical model reveals that for him history is a discourse that acts on the reader. Ultimately he wants to turn the reader into one of his group, into a political ally, in the same way that he turns the reader of the *Préface-annexe* into one of the conspirators. In this instance, he wants to turn the reader into an Enlightenment intellectual, into someone who can read critically and therefore draw his own conclusions about political events not just in the past but more significantly in the present.

But what happens if the reader refuses to engage in this process, if he adopts a negative position with respect to the Enlightenment *philosophes*? In effect, Diderot has already anticipated this possibility and has even countered its consequences. As he has implicitly shown us all along, there already exists in the past, in Seneca's text, the perfect model of the hostile reader, namely Seneca's detractors. And Diderot, as we have seen, has systematically dismantled their position. He delivers the coup de grâce when he observes: "We must admit that the enemies of our *philosophes* sometimes resemble Seneca's detractors marvelously" (179), thereby making very clear the analogy between Seneca's critics and the eighteenth-century *antiphilo-*

sophes, the enemies of Enlightenment, to whom Diderot refers throughout the *Essai* as *aristarques*.

The passage on the *aristarques* uncovers the final twist that Diderot gives to his structure. The first two instances of the ternary model were oriented toward the past: in one, the present was the starting point for moving toward the past; in the other, the past was the starting point for moving toward the present. In this instance, the past (both Diderot's past and Seneca's past) becomes the starting point to move toward the reader's present. Since the reader's present is always situated at a future remove from that of Diderot's act of writing, the temporal reversal that occurs here suggests that Diderot's ultimate concern is with posterity, with forming the future reader's perspective. More specifically, he wants to establish a particular image of himself for posterity, as is evident in the concluding sections of the *Essai*.

Just before the end of the *Essai*, Diderot reproduces his critics' objections both to the form and content of an earlier version of the *Essai* as well as to the ideas espoused by Diderot and other Enlightenment thinkers. He juxtaposes each objection with Marmontel's refutation of it. And, at certain moments, he interrupts the "dialogue" between the critics and Marmontel to intercalate his own remarks, which he prefaces with the phrase "And I will add that." To cite just one passage of this section of the *Essai*:

> [CRITICS] The author [of the *Essai*] is a terrible writer and the most awkward of apologists. . . .
> [MARMONTEL] We are of the opinion that the most precious philosophical monument we have left [Diderot's works] could not have been more worthily crowned than by this Essai; that it is full of passages of the greatest distinction in both the historical and apologetic genres; one recognizes in it the man of genius, the great writer, and the sensitive man.
> [DIDEROT] And *I will add* that of these three qualities, I only ac-

cept the last: it is enough for me. . . . If I happen to obtain the approbation of an honest and enlightened man like M. de Marmontel, I can feel flattered, but I cannot be vain about it. (407–8)

Two new terms—Diderot's critics and Marmontel—make an appearance here. Although the reader's inclusion is not explicit in the passage cited above, it is implicit, as Diderot reveals in the final pages of the *Essai*, where he addresses a series of questions directly to the reader. At first glance it might seem that the structure of the model has changed, but though there are now four terms instead of three, in fact it remains ternary, since Diderot and Marmontel, who both speak on Diderot's behalf, fulfill the same function and therefore occupy the same position in the circuit. What we have here, then, is a ternary model in which Diderot and Marmontel take a detour through Diderot's critics to approach the reader, in an attempt to discredit the critics' negative judgments of Diderot and his works. This is a *mise-en-abyme* of Diderot's own defense of Seneca in the preceding sections of the *Essai*. Moreover, this model resembles the Diderotian historical model in three different ways. First, it is again a conversational model (Diderot, Marmontel, and the critics carry on a "conversation" on paper); second, what is at stake in it is the particular effect Diderot wants to have on the reader; and, finally, it is also temporally oriented toward the future, and specifically toward posterity.

But Diderot is no longer discussing Seneca, the ancient Roman past, or even the Enlightenment—he is now explicitly speaking about himself. Furthermore, by reinforcing his own positions and views with Marmontel's defense of them, Diderot definitively shifts the focus of the *Essai* away from other concerns and instead places it squarely on himself. By so doing, he undermines the ostensible purpose of historical analysis. Whereas it appeared to be designed to give the reader the freedom to think for himself and to draw his own conclusions about events and people in the past and present, we now see Diderot using the model to fulfill his own ulterior motives. The model that the reader should have learned to recognize as a historical tool by the time he reaches the end of the *Essai* suddenly becomes an ideological tool instead, as it imposes on the reader the positive image of Diderot that Diderot would like future generations to retain. Indeed Diderot devotes several pages at the end of the *Essai* to singing his own praises. But the constraints Diderot builds into the concluding section of the *Essai* are most evident in the last two pages, where he addresses a series of questions to the reader.

These questions give the concluding section of the *Essai* the by now familiar appearance of an open-ended exchange. This time, however, the questions are rhetorical.

> [Reader], did [Diderot] speak of virtue as would a man who knows its sweetness and dignity, or as would a hypocrite rendered equally suspect by his conduct or by his writings?
> Am I an upstanding man, or a base apologist? And is my endeavor, whether successful or unsuccessful, worthy of praise or worthy of blame? (430)

Diderot thus makes it clear that he should go down in history as a virtuous man, consequent with his principles in his writings and his deeds, the victim of unfair accusations made by his intellectual and political opponents. In judging him, moreover, the reader should emulate the example he himself has set with respect to Seneca by refusing to believe those who have attacked him.

If we consider this picture of Diderot, we can see that it is his own image of himself that has functioned as the filter through which he has viewed Seneca and not just the reverse. This point allows us in turn to see the extent to which Diderot's notion of history has all along been idiosyncratic. For him history has less to do with the object of a historian's scrutiny than with the ways that posterity will be allowed to have access to the subject—and specifically to the historian. But Diderot's goal in writing the *Essai* is not to be the historian of himself in the same way that Suillius was the historian of Seneca. He seeks, rather, to do away with this model of history and the historian's work. He does not want, in other words, to be the positive counterpart of Suillius, to be the historian who will construct a positive image of Seneca for posterity; instead he wants to make historians' value judgments about past people irrelevant. To preclude the possibility that such judgments will be made, he replaces the traditional notion of history as a coherent and accurate account of subject or subject matter with the notion of history as activity, as process. The latter notion is implicit in Diderot's claim that he wrote the *Essai* not just to examine Seneca's life and works but also to: "avenge a great man, if he'd been slandered; or, if I thought him guilty, to lament his weaknesses and profit from his wise and powerful lessons" (35). Diderot's goal in writing the *Essai*, in other words, is to make it difficult for future generations to rely on preexisting judgments and to force them instead to interact with texts and documents, an activity that allows for change.

Diderot thus defines history not in terms of its object of study but in terms of activity. *One does not judge, one laments along with.* It is the actual mechanisms and conditions under which it is possible to engage in this kind of sympathetic interaction that are demonstrated in great detail in the *Rêve de d'Alembert*, the final text in my study of Diderot.

CHAPTER FIVE

PRELIMINARY DISCOURSES

NATURAL PHILOSOPHY IN D'ALEMBERT'S BOUDOIR

And note that in men's commerce there is nothing but noises and actions.

— Diderot, *Le Rêve de d'Alembert*

What is life, and how does living matter function? Throughout the *Rêve de d'Alembert* Diderot suggests that it functions like a system of communication. Interestingly enough, the model of communication we first discovered in the *Préface-annexe* of *La Religieuse* and subsequently traced in the rest of *La Religieuse* and in the *Essai sur les règnes de Claude et de Néron* reappears in what at first may seem an unlikely context: the conception of biological organization that Diderot explores in the *Rêve de d'Alembert*.[1] The *Préface-annexe* sets into motion a bifurcating, outwardly expanding circuit of communication, which, though repeatedly interrupted by the intrusion of outside terms, nevertheless escapes definitive disruption through the incorporation of these external terms into the circuit. In so doing, furthermore, the whole communicative circuit moves to a higher level of complexity.

With this model in mind, let us turn for a moment to one of the statements that d'Alembert makes in the course of his dream, as he recapitulates the content of an earlier exchange with Diderot: "A thread of very pure gold, I remember, is one simile he used; a homogeneous network among whose molecules others position themselves and perhaps form another homogeneous network, a tissue of sensate [*sensible*] matter, a contact that assimilates, some active sensibility [*sensibilité*] here, some inert sensibility there, which communicates itself like movement."[2] This description coincides almost exactly with the model of communication in the *Préface-annexe*. Besides the explicit use of the verb "to communicate" to describe the transmission of "active sensibility" from one molecule to another, other terms in the preceding passage — such as "network" and "contact" — also evoke the image of a circuit of communication. Moreover, this circuit, like the one in the *Préface-annexe*, is capable not only of integrating outside terms but also of using them to move to a higher level of complexity, for, as d'Alembert points out, the introduction of a different set of molecules between those already situated within a given network of molecules would potentially generate another such network.

Furthermore, in his recapitulation of Diderot's earlier statements, d'Alembert is careful to qualify the network of molecules he describes as "a tissue of sensate matter" and to note that what is transmitted from one molecule to another is "some active sensibility here, some inert sensibility there." This suggests that the key term in the elaboration of the analogy between communication and the functioning of biological systems is *sensibility*. To understand this crucial notion, however, it is necessary to take a close look at the beginning of the *Rêve de d'Alembert*, where the term *sensibility* makes its initial appearance.

The *Entretien entre Diderot et d'Alembert*, the first dialogue in the trilogy known collectively as the *Rêve de d'Alembert*, begins *in medias res*, with d'Alembert restating Diderot's arguments against the notion that God is the source of life and of all activity in the natural world. With this one move, Diderot destabilizes the philosophical foundation on which conventional explanations of life and of the workings of nature are built. For

Diderot, the notion of a God who is both part of nature and at the same time its exterior, controlling force, the notion of a being "that differs in essence from matter yet is one with it; that follows it and yet moves it without moving itself; that acts upon matter and yet undergoes all its vicissitudes" (89) is too contradictory to provide a coherent account of the origin and functioning of phenomena in the natural world.³ Such an account would instead have to be found in a principle or quality inherent to — and not in any way separate from — matter itself.⁴

To explain the phenomenon of life, therefore, Diderot turns to the notion of sensibility, which, according to the terms proposed at the beginning of the first dialogue, is "a general and essential quality of matter" (90). Diderot, however, neither describes nor defines sensibility further. It is only through an analysis of the passages in which the term appears that its meaning begins to emerge.

A section of the famous passage in the *Rêve* establishing an analogy between a harpsichord and a philosopher suggests that Diderot's use of the term *sensibility* draws on its strict acceptation and refers to the capacity to function through the senses: "We are instruments endowed with sensibility and memory. Our senses are so many keys that are struck [*pincées*, or plucked; the musical instrument Diderot is talking about actually plucks the strings rather than striking them] by surrounding nature, and that often strike themselves" (102). For Diderot, the senses are the receptors that open an organism to its environment. An entity possessing sensibility is therefore characteristically receptive to events taking place in its surroundings. Or as Diderot explicitly states in the *Eléments de physiologie*, sensibility is a "quality proper to animate beings that informs them of the relationships that exist between them and everything in their surroundings."⁵

But there is more than mere receptivity implicit in the notion of sensibility. Like harpsichords, which register the action of the player's fingers on their keys and respond to that action with a burst of music, entities that possess sensibility respond to environmental impressions with sounds. "In a harpsichord organized like you and me . . . there is an impression that has its cause either within the instrument or outside it, a sensation is born from this impression . . . and voices that designate them with natural or conventional sounds" (102–3). This description evokes a process of communication, for not only does nature enter into communication with living beings by "pressing" on their senses, but living beings in turn respond with utterances, themselves communicative acts. Entities possessing sensibility are therefore characterized not just by their receptivity to events in their surroundings but also by their capacity to respond to those events.

Furthermore, entities endowed with sensibility are receptive to a particular kind of environmental event, one that Diderot describes with the terms *impression* and *pincer*. *Impression* evokes not just its more abstract meaning of the "action that an object or feeling exerts on someone" but also its more literal meaning of the "action of leaving a mark, when speaking of one thing that presses on another."[6] This latter sense, which implies a physical disturbance or alteration, links it to Diderot's use of *pincer* in another important passage of the *Rêve de d'Alembert*.[7]

In the analogy Diderot draws between a harpsichord and a philosopher, the term *pincer* (which can mean both to pinch and to pluck) refers specifically to the action used to play a stringed instrument. But its other connotation, that of some kind of painful disturbance, also appears explicitly in the second dialogue of the *Rêve* when d'Alembert describes the impetus for the formation of a swarm of bees as the pinching of one bee by another: "If one of the bees [in the swarm] decides to pinch in some way the bee to which it has attached itself . . . the latter bee will pinch the next one . . . the whole swarm will go into motion, stir, change its position and shape . . . [and] noise will arise, little cries" (120–21). Each individual bee, when pinched, reacts by emitting little cries of pain ("noise," "little cries") and by repeating the same action ("the latter bee will pinch the next one"). Both *impression* and *pincer*, then, are linked to some kind of perturbation to which the entity possessing sensibility is receptive and to which it responds.

But in neither instance is the sensate entity's response immediate. Between the point at which the philosopher registers an impression and the point at which he responds to that impression with sounds (or, analogously, between the point at which the bees sense a pinch and the point at which they respond to that pinch with little noises), other crucial events intervene. Here, for instance, is what happens in the case of the philosopher.

> A sensation is born from [the first] impression, a sensation that has duration, for it is impossible to imagine that it could constitute and extinguish itself in an indivisible instant . . . another impression that succeeds [the first] and that also has its cause either within or outside the animal . . . a second sensation and voices that designate them with natural or conventional sounds. (103)

The intermediary step between the philosopher's registering of an impression and the pursuant response is something that Diderot calls sensation. With the term *sensation*, Diderot introduces duration ("a sensation . . . has duration, for it is impossible to imagine that it could constitute and extinguish itself in an indivisible instant"). The initial impression, in other words, continues to make itself felt in the sensate entity. To that first impression, furthermore, are added others ("another impression . . . succeeds [the first] and . . . [then] a second sensation") that in turn will elicit another set of sensations. Duration and succession thus become crucial catalysts in the process that the philosopher undergoes.

They are also catalysts in the process that the bees undergo. As we noted above, the initial pinch that any given bee registers subsequently elicits a succession of pinches: "If one of the bees [in the swarm] decides to pinch in some way the bee to which it has attached itself . . . the latter bee will pinch the next one" (120–21). And again, each pinch in turn provokes the lasting reverberations that Diderot calls sensations: "There will be aroused in the whole swarm as many sensations as there are small animals" (121).

Up to this point, what we have been observing is the unleashing of a process that follows inevitably from the sensate entity's reception of an impression. But we have yet to consider the results of this process. Let us therefore take a look at what happens to the bees after their initial response to an impression.

The process continues with a total rearrangement of the individual bees ("the whole swarm will go into motion, stir, change its position and shape" [121]) into the formation known as a bee swarm, which Diderot describes as looking like one animal with many different parts: "He who has never seen a similar swarm straightening itself out would be tempted to take it for an animal with five or six hundred heads and ten or twelve hundred wings" (120–21).[8] At this point, moreover, a new disturbance intervenes and takes the process one step further, changing the bee swarm from a conglomerate of individual parts into a single unified animal.

> Do you want to transform the bee swarm into a single unique animal? Smooth out the legs by which they hold on to each other; from the contiguous [entities] that they were, render them continuous. Between this new state of the swarm and the preceding one, there is certainly a marked difference; and what can this difference be, if not that at present it is a whole, a single animal, where before it was nothing more than an assemblage of animals? (121–22)

The dissolution of the bees' legs creates a new and different entity, no longer a disparate group but instead a complex cluster of bees that functions as if it were one organism. Thus what began as a seemingly simple interaction between the bees and their environment and between any two contiguous bees within the swarm, ends up producing an intricate communicative network among the bees in question and ultimately leads to the creation of a more complex entity.

The process that the philosopher undergoes evolves in a similar way. The initial impression that the philosopher registers becomes a sensation and eventually is converted into the sounds that he emits. But this is still only one step in a larger process; in turn the sounds that the philosopher emits become environmental disturbances or impressions for those living beings who may find themselves in his vicinity. The process of reception and response will thus be reinitiated, adding new participants to the network of communication and thereby increasing the complexity of the network.

So far the two examples we have analyzed—that of the philosopher who transforms impressions into sounds and that of the bees who fuse together to form a single unified animal—involve highly organized animate entities whose sensibility is generally agreed upon, since they quite literally possess sense organs. Diderot's claim in the *Rêve de d'Alembert*, however, is that sensibility is a general quality of matter. For such a statement to hold, it would be necessary to show that sensibility exists in inanimate as well as animate matter. Therefore, against the potential objection that it is impossible to ascribe sensibility to inanimate matter, Diderot makes a distinction between matter possessing inert sensibility and that possessing active sensibility and maintains that it is possible to effect a passage from the inert to the active state of sensibility. To lend weight to this hypothesis, he undertakes an elaborate demonstration to show how it is possible to make matter undergo this transformation.

He does this with the famous anecdote about Falconet's statue, which begins with Diderot imagining himself taking one of the sculptor's masterpieces and pulverizing it in a giant mortar. He describes to d'Alembert the rest of his hypothetical experiment.

> Once the block of marble has been reduced to an impalpable powder, I mix that powder with humus, or loam; I knead them well together; I water the mixture and let it putrefy for a year, two years, a century, time is of no concern. When the whole has been transformed into more or less homogeneous matter, into humus . . . I sow peas, beans, cabbages, and other leguminous plants. The plants nourish themselves with the soil, and I nourish myself with the plants. (94–95)

Diderot's account of the process that Falconet's statue undergoes as it is transformed from an inert, "dead" representation of a human being into an active, "live" component of a human body follows the same pattern as the transformation of perturbations or impressions into sounds. The statue's metamorphosis begins with a severe disturbance that changes its original form: the pounding that reduces it to a fine powder. This procedure allows the particles of marble to come into contact with a different kind of substance, "humus or loam." Once they have been put into such close physical proximity to each other, the particles of humus, which presumably are sensate, interact with and interpenetrate the particles of marble, which are not. As a result, the mixture undergoes a process of assimilation, both in the sense of incorporation, as the "living" particles of humus ingest the "dead" particles of marble, and in the sense of making similar, as the particles of marble become *like* the particles of humus. They are transformed, in Diderot's words, into "more or less homogeneous matter."

At this point, however, the statue's metamorphosis is not yet complete. Diderot goes on to plant seeds in the soil formed from the mixture of humus and minute particles of marble.

The soil then nourishes the seeds, from which new plants are eventually born. Finally, the process of making marble sensate will be complete when human beings eat the new plants, for as Diderot remarks at a different point, eating is a common, daily activity whereby we transform matter whose sensibility is inert into matter whose sensibility is active (93).

What Diderot manages to "prove" with this demonstration is not so much that marble is inherently sensate, or even that the most minute particles of matter possess sensibility, but more precisely that sensibility can be communicated from one substance to another. Although this claim remains implicit in the Falconet episode, it is stated explicitly in the second dialogue of the *Rêve* by d'Alembert, who, while dreaming and reviewing Diderot's statements in the first dialogue, murmurs, "Just as a drop of mercury melts into another drop of mercury, so a molecule that is sensate and living melts into a molecule that is sensate and living" (118). And further on: "a tissue of sensate matter, a contact that assimilates, some active sensibility here, some inert sensibility there, which communicates itself like movement" (119). When a substance that possesses active sensibility comes into contact with one that possesses inert sensibility, the former transmits its particular kind of sensibility to the latter. In the *Rêve de d'Alembert*, then, sensibility refers both to the capacity to enter into communication with other elements in nature (and as such marks the beginning of a process) and also the end result of that process, as entities that previously lacked active sensibility acquire it through contact with other entities that already possess it.[9]

If we now reconsider Diderot's account of the creation of sounds from impressions, of a bee swarm from individual bees, and of flesh from marble, it becomes clear that these successive metamorphoses are a product of the communication through contact that sensibility makes possible. Moreover, each metamorphosis traces a passage from simpler organizations toward organizations of ever-increasing complexity, and even from nonliving matter to living matter, thereby suggesting that contact among entities possessing sensibility plays a crucial role in nature's generative processes.

Indeed this notion is stated explicitly at various points throughout the *Rêve de d'Alembert*. In one instance, Mademoiselle de l'Espinasse claims that human reproduction begins when the "seminal fluids" of two people come into contact with each other: "a machine as complex as an animal . . . is born . . . perhaps of two fluids mixed together by chance" (150). But possibly the best example of the role of contact in generative processes can be found in Diderot's description of the process of eating: "When you eat, what do you do? You lift the obstacles that opposed the active sensibility of the nutriment. You assimilate it with yourself; you turn it into flesh; you animalize it; you render it sensate" (93). The action of eating, which at first creates a disruption in the conformation of the substance being eaten, subsequently eliminates the "obstacles that opposed the active sensibility of the nutriment" by putting the nutriment into contact with a living being that possesses active sensibility. The substance that has been ingested next undergoes assimilation ("you assimilate it with yourself"), and the end result of the whole process is the creation of something new—flesh—where before there was nothing more than a "nutriment."

Not surprisingly, then, Diderot ends up explicitly designating eating as the prototype of generative processes. He does this in an ironic description of d'Alembert's gradual transformation from an embryo into a great mathematician.

> And thus you have that rare germ formed; here you have him led through the fallopian tubes into the uterus, as common opinion has it; here you have him attached to the uterus by a long pedicle; here you have him growing successively and advancing toward the fetal state; here you have the moment arrive for its exit from

the dark prison; here you have him born, exposed on the steps of Saint-Jean-le-rond, which gave him his name; taken from the orphanage; attached to the breast of good Madame Rousseau, the glazier's wife; suckled, he has become great in body and mind, a man of letters, a practitioner of the science of mechanics, a geometer. How did all this come about? Through eating and other purely mechanical operations. (96)

To the question of how d'Alembert the adult evolved from a fertilized egg, Diderot proposes the answer, "Through eating and other purely mechanical operations," thereby underscoring the generative role he attributes to the process of alimentation.[10]

Furthermore, Diderot's insistence on the role of "purely mechanical operations" in the process of gestation underscores his desire to dissociate the issue of genesis from its theological context and to establish instead that the organization of living beings and the functioning of the natural world can be ascribed not to the will of God but rather to the independent activity of a nature devoid of God. This is a point that he makes explicitly when he tells d'Alembert that "whoever would lecture the Academy on the progress of the formation of a man or an animal would only do so in terms of material agents whose successive effects would be an inert being, a feeling being, a thinking being, a being finding the solution to the problem of the precession of the equinoxes, a sublime being, a marvelous being, an aging being, wasting away, dying, decomposed and returned to loam" (96). He then goes on to propose a somewhat facetious "formula" for such a material genesis: "Eat, digest, distill *in vasi licito, et fiat homo secundum artem* [in a legitimate vessel, and let there be man by artificial means]" (96).

Remarkably, the three steps that Diderot outlines in this formula parallel the successive steps in the other generative processes that he had previously described: the transformation of marble into flesh, impressions into sounds, and individual bees into a bee swarm. In each of these instances, the first step in the transformation was a disturbance that put two or more substances that were previously separated into contact with each other ("eat"); the second an assimilative process that took place over time ("digest"); and the third the creation of a new and different entity ("distill"). A schema of these analogous processes would look like this:

"eat"	pulverization	pluck	pinch
"digest"	putrefaction	sensation	sensations
"distill"	plant (flesh)	sound	bee swarm

But Diderot's formula elides a factor that plays a crucial role in the metamorphoses outlined above, though other passages in the *Rêve* either allude to its role in generative processes or explicitly describe it. That factor is time. At various points in the *Rêve*, Diderot has his characters comment on the role of time in generative processes. In one instance, Bordeu observes: "Nature [brings] about over time everything that is possible" (163). This notion echoes one of the statements that the character Diderot made in the first dialogue while speculating about the effects of time on human evolution: "Grant man not immortality but merely twice his lifetime, and you'll see what will come of it" (113). In both passages, however, Diderot is careful not to make any claims about the specific results of the natural processes in which time plays an activating role. This is because in his view, the passage of time will bring with it not only changes and new events but more specifically changes and new events that cannot be predicted, effects that cannot be deduced from a given cause. As the character Diderot states in the first dialogue of the *Rêve*: "The cause undergoes too many particular vicissitudes that escape us for us to count infallibly on the effect that will ensue" (110).

An echo of this statement appears later in the *Rêve* when

Bordeu observes that it is impossible to deduce future events from those taking place in the present.

> If man isn't separated out into an infinity of men, he separates out, at least, into an infinity of animalcules whose future and final metamorphoses and organization are impossible to foresee. Who knows if this might not be the seedbed of a second generation of beings, removed from this one by an unfathomable interval of centuries and successive developments? (126)

Diderot, furthermore, claims that the reverse is also true, that there are no causal links between the present and the past. As the character Diderot states in the first dialogue:

> If the question of which came first, the chicken or the egg, stymies you, it is because you assume that animals at their origins were what they are at present. What folly! We have no more idea of what they have been than we do of what they will become. (97–98)

According to the terms that Diderot proposes in the *Rêve de d'Alembert*, then, time is an essential ingredient in processes that produce radically new and unpredictable events and phenomena in nature.

If we now reconsider Diderot's hypothesis from the beginning of the first dialogue of the *Rêve*, we can begin to see why he believes that sensibility can substitute for God as the source of life and of activity in the natural world. By putting living entities into contact with other entities and other objects in their surroundings, sensibility creates communicative links among the various components of the natural world, links that allow them to interact with each other.[11] This notion is stated explicitly, again by d'Alembert, in the second dialogue, when he speculates: "There must be some difference between the contact of two molecules that are sensate and the contact of two molecules that are not; and this difference, what can it be? . . . a habitual action and reaction" (119).

Instead of a nature that acts through God, then, Diderot describes a nature that interacts or, to use the terms that we have been adopting throughout, a nature that communicates, thanks to the sensibility of its constituent parts. What this functional principle permits Diderot to describe is a secular genesis, secular because it no longer has a theological basis and also because its activating element is time. This secular genesis, furthermore, follows a series of well-defined steps that can be traced not just in the biological processes that Diderot describes in the *Rêve de d'Alembert* but also in the rhetorical structure of its three dialogues.

One of the most distinctive features of the *Rêve de d'Alembert* is that the interaction among the various interlocutors in the three dialogues parallels its descriptions of generative processes in nature. Like the bee swarm, whose members come together, form a whole, and then separate, the conversation that begins in the first dialogue and ends in the third also has shifting configurations of interlocutors. In the first dialogue the interlocutors are Diderot and d'Alembert, in the second Mademoiselle de l'Espinasse and Bordeu, with d'Alembert at times either talking in his sleep or joining the conversation, and in the third dialogue d'Alembert disappears altogether, leaving Mademoiselle and Bordeu to carry on the exchange.

Like genesis in nature, furthermore, the conversation itself is a process that takes place across a long interval of time. Diderot highlights this trait of the conversation by having the interlocutors frequently refer to the time that is passing. For example, at the end of the first third of the second dialogue, we learn that it is very early in the morning when d'Alembert wakes up momentarily and, before lapsing back to sleep, says to Bordeu: "Good morning, Doctor, what are you doing here at such an early hour?" (144) At a later point, d'Alembert again wakes up briefly and asks, "Did I dream?" Mademoiselle answers: "All night long" (163), thereby underscoring the length of time that d'Alembert's dream has lasted. Mademoiselle makes this comment shortly after Bordeu has noted that it is already midmorning: "It is half past ten [in the morning] and I hear a patient calling me from the outskirts of town" (163). Moreover, just before the second dialogue ends, Bordeu points out that yet another hour has gone by: "It is half past eleven, and at noon I have a consultation in the Marais" (192). The final indication of the passage of time comes at the beginning of the third dialogue, when we are told that it is now two o'clock in the afternoon (195). Thus the conversation that had begun the previous evening lasts until at least mid-afternoon of the following day.

But there are more specific resemblances in the *Rêve de d'Alembert* between the biological phenomena it describes and its rhetorical structure. This is an appropriate place to turn to an analysis of the process whereby one group of interlocutors (Diderot and Bordeu, the "believers") attempts to persuade the other group (d'Alembert and Mademoiselle de l'Espinasse, the "skeptics") of the validity of the ideas that the character Diderot proposes in the first dialogue.

At the beginning of the first dialogue of the *Rêve*, as noted earlier, Diderot substitutes for the theological explanation of life and the workings of nature the notion of sensibility. Throughout the ensuing dialogue, Diderot reasons with d'Alembert, trying to win him over to his point of view. All his efforts, however, are in vain. D'Alembert steadfastly refuses to endorse Diderot's hypotheses. Nevertheless, d'Alembert's stubbornness is not enough to deter Diderot. Realizing that his appeals to d'Alembert's reason are bound to be ineffective, he tries a different approach. This approach uses the biological model described earlier. To make d'Alembert "see reason," Diderot will attempt to activate his sensibility. As we saw previously, the way to do this is to create an environmental disturbance that will affect d'Alembert's senses, establish contact between d'Alembert and another entity that possesses active sensibility, and then allow the interaction between the two to evolve over time.

Without d'Alembert's realizing it, this is precisely what has been taking place all along. As if d'Alembert were a living analogue of Falconet's statue, in the course of the first dialogue Diderot places him in a "mortar" and "pulverizes" him by dispensing with the notion of God as the source of life and of all activity in the natural world.[12] This notion is the cornerstone of the classical epistemology to which d'Alembert subscribes, and as a result Diderot's statements are nothing more than disordered sounds for d'Alembert. Nevertheless, d'Alembert's resistance allows Diderot (an entity whose sensibility is already active) to prolong contact with d'Alembert (an entity whose sensibility is currently inert) for, greatly disturbed by Diderot's hypotheses, d'Alembert insistently continues his attempts to refute them. D'Alembert's resistance, however, operates only on the level of the intellectual argument, for he has already been acted upon on a different level. The sounds Diderot has been emitting as he argues have literally entered d'Alembert's body and have altered the state of his molecules.[13] By reasoning with d'Alembert, therefore, Diderot has merely been employing a diversionary tactic designed to allow the effects of the sounds that have reached d'Alembert to take hold.

By the end of the first dialogue, there is evidence that Diderot's strategy has been effective. Before their discussion draws to a close, d'Alembert suddenly announces to Diderot that he is tired and is going home to bed: "Farewell, my friend, good night and sleep well" (111). As it turns out, Diderot's pronouncements have indeed begun to affect d'Alembert. But instead of affecting his mind—his faculty of reason—they have affected his body, as his precipitous fatigue suggests. The inevitable consequence of their discussion is that d'Alembert will fall asleep. This physiological change in d'Alembert, furthermore, is the factor that will ultimately make him move from a state of inert sensibility to a state of active sensibility. For sleep, as we discover at another point in the second dialogue, activates sensibility: "During waking hours the network obeys the impressions coming from the exterior object. During sleep, it is from the exercise of its own sensibility that everything happening within it emanates" (183). Thus, although d'Alembert seems to be under the impression that by going home to bed he will escape the disturbing discussion with Diderot, he has merely played into Diderot's hands. This is all the more true since d'Alembert's fatigue subsequently makes him lose his appetite and eventually gives him a fever, physiological disorders that in turn make him dream while he sleeps. This is all part of Diderot's game plan: the process of dreaming will provide the temporal development necessary for the full effects of the sounds that have entered d'Alembert's body to take hold. Therefore, to increase the probabilities that this will indeed happen, Diderot, in parting, assures d'Alembert that as soon as he goes to sleep he will dream about what Diderot has said: "You will dream on your pillow about this conversation, and if it doesn't acquire any consistency there, too bad for you, as you will be forced to embrace far more ridiculous hypotheses" (111). However, by the time Diderot makes this statement, he is merely pointing out the inevitable consequences of the situation he has already prepared during the course of the first dialogue. For despite d'Alembert's attempts to interrupt the communication with Diderot, their exchange will continue from the moment d'Alembert begins to dream.

And at this point the tables are turned once again. The changes in d'Alembert's body in turn produce changes in his intellectual perspective. This is evident in the words he speaks at the beginning of his dream. Whereas in the first dialogue d'Alembert had actively opposed Diderot's proposals, in the dream he adopts both positions. He reiterates some of his arguments against Diderot's hypotheses (identified in Mademoiselle de l'Espinasse's transcript of this part of the dream by the pronoun "I" and by the apostrophes to the "philosopher"), but he also reiterates parts of Diderot's defense of his own hypotheses (identified in the transcript at one point by the apostrophe "My friend d'Alembert" and by the pronoun "he," as when d'Alembert says, "[This] is one simile he used" or "as he himself said so well" [119]). The reprocessing that takes place during the course of d'Alembert's dream thus creates a closer, more effective form of contact with Diderot's ideas than their verbal exchange had.

And as the dream progresses—although there are still moments when d'Alembert seems to be repeating almost verbatim what Diderot had said in the first dialogue—the distinctions between the subjective and objective viewpoints gradually fade away. The markers that had served to distinguish Diderot's points from d'Alembert's in earlier sections of the dream ("he," "you," "philosopher") disappear, and now d'Alembert speaks in the first person, no longer attributing what he is saying to Diderot. It is as if in the course of the various presentations and re-presentations of Diderot's arguments a shift were made from direct discourse (as, for example, when d'Alembert quotes Diderot), to indirect discourse (as, for example, when d'Alembert relates in his own words the substance of some of Diderot's statements while still attributing them to Diderot), and finally to a common discourse, where the original source of an idea or statement has been "forgotten" and can no longer be identified.

A striking instance of this fusion appears toward the end of Mademoiselle de l'Espinasse's account of d'Alembert's dream, when d'Alembert exclaims: "Having seen inert matter pass to the state of sensibility, nothing should ever again astonish me" (131), a statement that echoes one of Diderot's points from the first dialogue but which is now formulated by d'Alembert as if it were his own. It is, furthermore, an apt description of the very process that d'Alembert himself has undergone. Having now experienced the passage from one state of sensibility to another, d'Alembert is finally able to acknowledge that the phenomenon exists.

D'Alembert's gradual internalization of Diderot's ideas is analogous to the first two steps in the generative processes Diderot described in the first dialogue, namely, ingestion and assimilation. First d'Alembert "ingests" Diderot's hypotheses, and subsequently he assimilates them. That he has done so is evident in the observations he begins to make, observations whose underlying assumptions coincide with Diderot's. Dreaming, therefore, is the psychic equivalent of eating; it is a process that removes from d'Alembert's mind the "obstacles that opposed [his] active sensibility" (93).

Moreover, there is yet another factor that contributes to the efficacy of d'Alembert's "ingestion" of Diderot's ideas. Like its analogue in nature, d'Alembert's assimilation of Diderot's ideas is a process that takes place over time, for d'Alembert's dream lasts throughout an entire night and continues into the following morning. And it is not until almost noon of that day — the time that marks the end of the second dialogue — that final proof is given that a persuasion has been operated. At this point, after a brief exchange with Bordeu, d'Alembert exclaims: "Very well, here we have everything brought back to sensibility, memory, organic movements; that suits me rather well" (188). These are precisely the arguments he had rejected in the first dialogue, but which he can now accept not just while he is asleep but also when he is fully awake. Thus it is both the contact that d'Alembert has had with an entity who is in a state of active sensibility and the prolongation of that contact through his dream that ultimately accounts for the transformation in d'Alembert's intellectual perspective.

A parallel development takes place in Mademoiselle de l'Espinasse, during the course of an exchange with the sleeping d'Alembert.[14] Worried by d'Alembert's unusual behavior upon his return from his appointment with Diderot, Mademoiselle de l'Espinasse decides to spend the whole night by his bedside. D'Alembert, who by now is in the throes of an acute state of active sensibility, suffering from a slight fever and furiously dreaming about his discussion with Diderot, talks in his sleep as a consequence of his condition. What he says, however, is totally incomprehensible to Mademoiselle. In the same way that Diderot's hypotheses were mere sounds for d'Alembert in the first dialogue, d'Alembert's utterings are "noise" for Mademoiselle. She herself points this out when she uses the terms "gibberish" (116), "incoherent musings" (116; 124), and "ramblings" (122) to describe them.

At this point, Mademoiselle's inability to comprehend suggests that she, like d'Alembert before her, is currently in a state of inert sensibility. But the contact she has already had with d'Alembert, who is now in a state of active sensibility, in addition to the exposure she has had to the sounds he is emitting, very quickly begin to change this situation. And they do so in an unusual way.

Mademoiselle responds to d'Alembert's condition and to her increasing concern about it by transcribing mechanically everything that d'Alembert is saying. Her doing so is a sign that "noise" is affecting Mademoiselle's body. Although one would think the contrary, that by writing down d'Alembert's speeches she is engaging in an intellectual activity that will organize them for her and thus give her mastery over their content, this in fact is not the case. Mademoiselle is merely going through the motions of tracing words on a page, without understanding what she is writing, as she herself admits to Bordeu: "My word, Doctor, I so little understood what I was writing" (123).

To her great dismay, furthermore, she can make no sense

whatsoever of what d'Alembert has said even after she has finished writing down his speeches and reread her transcript. Once transcribed, in other words, the "noise" of d'Alembert's utterings does not become "message." Instead, its unintelligibility is reproduced literally in Mademoiselle's transcript, as she indicates by calling it her "scribblings" (124), and a portion of which she describes as being "so blurred that I cannot read it" (123). In the case of Mademoiselle, therefore, the act of transcribing is a *physical* reaction analogous to the sleepiness and fever that Diderot's words had produced in d'Alembert at the end of the first dialogue. The process through which she will eventually acquire active sensibility is beginning to take effect.

And sure enough, by morning Mademoiselle is at least as agitated, if not more, than d'Alembert was during the course of his dream.[15] At this point, she becomes so alarmed by what she is experiencing and by her fear that d'Alembert may be gravely ill that she calls in Bordeu, d'Alembert's doctor, for a consultation.

Mademoiselle then reads her transcript of d'Alembert's dream aloud to Bordeu, thus reviving the sonority of the silent graphic disorder of her text. Bordeu also gives voice to Mademoiselle's text, when, having guessed what d'Alembert must have said during the night, he exhorts Mademoiselle to look at the sheet of paper in her hand and listen to him. To her great amazement, he proceeds to "read" aloud the words that Mademoiselle had earlier transcribed on the page.[16] Moreover, at various times during the second dialogue d'Alembert intermittently takes up the thread of his dream and again talks in his sleep. Consequently, in the same way that d'Alembert's dream had allowed him both to review and prolong his conversation with Diderot, the events of the second dialogue intensify and prolong Mademoiselle's exposure to what she perceives as mere noise emanating from d'Alembert.

Gradually, however, the process that had begun while Mademoiselle was transcribing d'Alembert's dream and that is now repeated as she reviews her transcript goes into its final stages and begins to have the by now predictable results. Although Mademoiselle de l'Espinasse had repeatedly protested throughout the first third of the second dialogue of the *Rêve* that d'Alembert's statements were "ravings that are only heard in the madhouse" (125) and that Bordeu was also "insane" (121) for agreeing with him, as the dialogue progresses she suddenly catches herself thinking in the same way as Bordeu: "I've just had a crazy idea indeed" (152). Though Mademoiselle may still qualify the new ideas that come to her as being crazy, she no longer sees them as being nothing more than meaningless sound.

Similarly, although at first d'Alembert is the only one who dreams, Mademoiselle and Bordeu at one point become so engrossed in one of Bordeu's arguments that they both lapse into a reverie; in an aside, it is mentioned that "after a fairly long silence, Mademoiselle de l'Espinasse emerged from her reverie and roused the doctor from his with [a] question" (152). Moreover, at another point in the second dialogue, Mademoiselle, who is becoming increasingly involved in the conversation with Bordeu, suggests that the spider and its web could be an apt metaphor for the human nervous system.

> Imagine a spider at the center of its web . . . if a particle makes one of the threads in the spider's web oscillate, [the spider] then takes alarm, it becomes restless, it runs in and out. At its center it is informed about everything that happens in any given part of the immense apartment it has woven. (141)

Bordeu immediately compliments Mademoiselle by pointing out the resemblance between her metaphor and d'Alembert's metaphor of the bees. This indication of the growing similarities between her utterances and d'Alembert's takes Mademoiselle by surprise and she exclaims: "Ah, that's true; I spoke prose without realizing it" (141). Mademoiselle's metaphor also provides an apt description of her own current state, for, like the spider, she is in the process of reacting to the "particles" that have struck her—in the form of d'Alembert's and Bordeu's words.

Finally, toward the end of the second dialogue, Mademoiselle stops and says "Just a moment, Doctor, let us recapitulate" (188) and then not only restates some of Bordeu's points but also uses an example to illustrate them, thus demonstrating that she has finally perceived structure in what she had previously described as "gibberish."

Like Mademoiselle, let us stop for a moment and recapitulate. In each of the conversations we have looked at so far, the one recurrent factor is noise, the third term that always intervenes in the circuit of communication between any two interlocutors. In all three conversations, moreover, the noise always takes the form of spoken words—first Diderot's hypotheses, then d'Alembert's speeches, and finally Mademoiselle's reading of her transcript. But it is not the semantic content of Diderot's utterances that affects d'Alembert, nor the semantic content of d'Alembert's utterances that affects Mademoiselle. As we saw earlier, both d'Alembert and Mademoiselle are immune to this aspect of Diderot's (and subsequently d'Alembert's) pronouncements. Rather, they are affected quite literally by the *sounds* of the words themselves, sounds that physically strike the eardrum, thereby entering their bodies and inducing a state of active sensibility in the interlocutors. Bordeu describes this process as follows:

> If a touching word strikes the ear of a sensate being, if an unusual phenomenon strikes its eye, then suddenly everything is thrown into a tumult, all the strands of the bundle are agitated, a shudder spreads throughout them, horror takes hold, tears flow, sobs suf-

focate, the voice cracks, the origin of the bundle does not know what will become of it. (179)

This state, where sensibility dominates, in turn allows the interlocutors to begin to understand and assimilate the semantic content of the utterances that had at first been incomprehensible to them.[17]

In the *Rêve*, then, communication takes place not through reason but through sensibility. Communication, in other words, does not function *directly* on the intellectual level but rather *indirectly* by first taking a detour through the body in order to reach the mind. But this process can make sense only if we understand that for Diderot there is no distinction between mind and matter, as he explicitly affirms in the first dialogue of the *Rêve*:

> D'ALEMBERT You have a grudge against the distinction between the two substances.
> DIDEROT I make no secret of that. (102)

It is only because in his view mind and matter are not distinct from each other that Diderot can maintain that understanding takes place materially.[18] Throughout the *Rêve*, therefore, Diderot defines communication as a material process whereby matter (sounds) enters into contact with matter (a body), changing both the body (its sensibility) and the mind (its capacity to understand).

In the second dialogue, however, Diderot gives an even more literal interpretation to this physical process of communication. More is at stake in the *Rêve* than the mere acquisition of active sensibility. To understand what is taking place, however, we must first examine the role that Bordeu plays in increasing Mademoiselle's receptivity to d'Alembert's ideas. For this we must turn to the beginning of the second dialogue, the point at which Bordeu makes his first appearance.

Before Bordeu's arrival on the scene, d'Alembert has caught

active sensibility from Diderot and Mademoiselle has caught it from d'Alembert. As a result, both have already begun to experience its effects. And although Bordeu has been called in to take care of d'Alembert, he determines almost immediately after arriving that d'Alembert is not seriously ill: "It is a slight touch of fever that won't have any serious consequences" (116). Mademoiselle's condition, however, is an altogether different matter. She is extremely agitated and excessively anxious about the state of d'Alembert's health. Furthermore, despite Bordeu's reassurances to the contrary, she continues to protest that d'Alembert is ill and that the statements he has made throughout the night are the ravings of a madman. Consequently, it rapidly becomes clear to Bordeu that Mademoiselle is in greater need of his care than d'Alembert. We can assume that Bordeu has correctly diagnosed Mademoiselle's "disease," for as we saw earlier, Bordeu is familiar with the causes and symptoms of extreme cases of sensibility (179). He therefore launches into a vehement defense of d'Alembert's ideas, believing that reason is the best antidote to Mademoiselle's seemingly irrational agitation and skepticism. It does not take long for Bordeu to choose his tactic: he will help Mademoiselle by pitting reason against sensibility.

Using his knowledge of nature and biology, Bordeu reviews the principal points in d'Alembert's speeches and tries to convince Mademoiselle that they are both rational and coherent. And, as we have already seen, although at first Mademoiselle resists Bordeu's attempts to reason with her, she gradually cedes and finds herself going along with his arguments. At first sight, then, it appears that reason has won its battle against sensibility.

However, in the course of the second dialogue an interesting reversal takes place. Although Bordeu is presumably the one who is trying to effect a change in Mademoiselle, his "patient" and interlocutor, it gradually becomes clear that Mademoiselle is starting to have a rather strange effect on *him*. As the conversation evolves, Bordeu finds it increasingly difficult to escape her clutches. About halfway through the second dialogue, for example, he announces that he must depart because another patient is waiting for him: "It is half past ten [in the morning], and I hear a patient calling me from the outskirts of town" (163). Mademoiselle, however, cleverly convinces him to stay. Having already understood that Bordeu prefers whenever possible not to interfere with nature's own healing process, she formulates a question whose answer, as she correctly calculates, will force him to play into her hands:

> MADEMOISELLE Would there be much danger [for the patient] if you didn't see him?
> BORDEU Less, perhaps, than if I do. If nature doesn't do the work without me, we shall have a great deal of difficulty doing it together, and I most certainly won't be able to do it without her.
> MADEMOISELLE Stay then. (163)

Mademoiselle turns the tables on Bordeu and convinces him to stay by using one of his most dearly held medical principles against him. Shortly thereafter, Bordeu once again tries to interrupt the conversation, insisting that he simply does not have time to explore the implications of a point that he has just made. Here again Mademoiselle persuades him to stay by pointing out to him that he has already missed his appointment: "But Doctor, the time for your visit has gone by, and your patient will no longer be waiting for you" (169).

It is at this point that Bordeu begins to realize that he is no longer free to extricate himself from the conversation, that he is now at the mercy of Mademoiselle's incessant questions and enticements to continue his arguments. He responds to this situation by testily telling Mademoiselle: "One should come here only when one has nothing else to do, for one can never get away" (169). Nevertheless, unperturbed by Bordeu's complaint, Mademoiselle again manages to goad him on: "There's a totally understandable outburst of temper; but your stories?" (169). With this question, which will later be echoed in the incessant requests that the Master makes to Jacques for the story of his "loves," Mademoiselle launches Bordeu on a topic whose exposition will require another hour of discussion. Clearly, Mademoiselle has learned to use her incomprehension strategically. It allows her to prolong her conversation with Bordeu, for the longer she refuses to accept that d'Alembert's statements are coherent and rational (or in other words, the longer the noise remains in the circuit), the longer Bordeu must argue with her.

Subsequently, however, Mademoiselle stops resisting and begins to follow Bordeu's line of reasoning. Her doing so is not just a sign that she has begun to accept the ideas that she had previously rejected but also, and perhaps more important, a sign that Mademoiselle has now learned what to say in order to keep up the conversation with Bordeu. Indeed Mademoiselle now takes an active, rather than a passive, role in the conversation; she actively follows Bordeu's line of reasoning, encourages him to continue, and asks him pointed questions about his arguments again and again. These strategies, however, are not altogether innocent; she uses them as a way of buying time, of prolonging the exchange with Bordeu. And all for a very specific reason: the longer Mademoiselle can manage to keep Bordeu in d'Alembert's bedroom, the longer Bordeu will be in contact with not just one but two entities (Mademoiselle and d'Alembert) who are both in a state of active sensibility. And the longer this contact lasts, the greater the chances that Bordeu too will move from an inert to an active state of sensibility.

In the same way that Diderot had earlier reasoned with d'Alembert as a means of distracting him from the physical changes he was beginning to undergo, so Mademoiselle actively encourages Bordeu to theorize to prevent him from becoming aware of the changes occurring in his physical state. And once again, Mademoiselle ends up using Bordeu's knowledge against him. She intuitively uses as a diversionary tactic a phenomenon that Bordeu understands in purely intellectual terms, but which he does not yet realize that he is experiencing. Ironically, it is Bordeu himself who at one point in their conversation explains the premise of Mademoiselle's strategy.

> A philosopher . . . had been tormented by an earache for fifteen days . . . he thought that his only recourse was to trick the pain through artifice. Little by little he became so engrossed in a problem of metaphysics or geometry that he forgot his ear. . . . The horrible pain began again only when the mental exertion ended. (173–74)

By Bordeu's own account, intense intellectual activity prevents the mind from being aware of what is happening to the body. For this very reason, Bordeu's ability to understand Mademoiselle's operational principle does not keep him from falling into her trap.

In the second dialogue, therefore, Mademoiselle ends up giving Bordeu a taste of his own medicine. Although the dialogue had begun with Bordeu administering a dose of reason to Mademoiselle as a means of curing her attack of sensibility, as the conversation evolves Mademoiselle more cleverly uses reason as a way of activating Bordeu's sensibility. Mademoiselle, in other words, manages to collapse the distinction between reason and sensibility by using one to distract the other. Her medicine, moreover, proves to be more powerful than Bordeu's, for he gradually begins to exhibit some of the same symptoms of sensibility as d'Alembert. Besides the increasing difficulty he has in extricating himself from the web Mademoiselle has woven around him, another important sign of the change in Bordeu is that his discourse and thoughts begin to fuse with Mademoiselle's, just as d'Alembert's had fused with Diderot's once he had begun to acquire active sensibility.

Indeed there are moments in the second dialogue when Mademoiselle and Bordeu seem able to read each other's minds.

At one point, Bordeu guesses what Mademoiselle is about to say:

> MADEMOISELLE But here is another extravagant idea that comes to me.
> BORDEU I exempt you from saying it, I know what it is.
> . . . .
> MADEMOISELLE You've guessed it. (143)

But the most striking instance of this phenomenon occurs when Mademoiselle is searching for the name of a person whose case history she wants to cite as an example of the physiological effects produced by a blow to the head: "A young man, about eighteen to twenty years old, whose name I don't remember" (167). With only the young man's age as a clue, Bordeu performs the impossible feat of providing the name: "He's a certain M. Schullemberg de Winterthour; he was only about fifteen to sixteen years old" (167). Mademoiselle de l'Espinasse forgets the name and Bordeu "remembers" it, an accomplishment all the more uncanny as Mademoiselle had gotten the young man's age wrong.

This uncanny complementarity between Bordeu's thoughts and Mademoiselle's is reflected, at another point, in the structure of their exchange. Here again Bordeu seems to know what Mademoiselle is going to say before she says it and can therefore speak in her stead.

> MADEMOISELLE It has seemed to me several times while dreaming . . .
> BORDEU And to those undergoing an attack of gout . . .
> MADEMOISELLE That I was becoming immense.
> BORDEU That their feet were touching the canopy of their beds.
> MADEMOISELLE That my arms and legs were stretching out to infinity. (157)

In this section of the dialogue, Mademoiselle's discourse and Bordeu's literally become intertwined; Mademoiselle de l'Espinasse begins a sentence, and its subsequent relative clauses are provided alternately by her and by Bordeu, as if just one person were speaking.

However, what is most interesting about the increasing interpenetration of Mademoiselle's and Bordeu's thoughts and discourse is that this process parallels what is happening between them on the physical level. As the second dialogue progresses, it becomes increasingly clear that more is at stake in the physical interaction between the two interlocutors than Bordeu's acquisition of active sensibility.

The earliest indication of what is at stake in the process that d'Alembert, Mademoiselle, and Bordeu each undergoes can be found in Mademoiselle's description of d'Alembert's agitation while he dreams. Once he is fully in the throes of active sensibility, Mademoiselle observes the following behavior:

> Then his face reddened. I wanted to feel his pulse, but I don't know where he'd concealed his hand. He seemed to be experiencing a convulsion. His mouth was half-opened; he was breathing quickly; he let out a deep sigh, and then a sigh that was more faint yet deeper still; he turned his head the other way on the pillow and fell asleep. (129)

The spectacle of the masturbating d'Alembert elicits an intense physical and emotional response in Mademoiselle: "I was watching him attentively, and I was deeply moved without knowing why, my heart was beating fast, and it wasn't from fear" (129).[19] Thus by the time Bordeu arrives on the scene, Mademoiselle has experienced the very specific physical consequences of the state of active sensibility and is now ready to prepare a repeat performance with Bordeu.

Indeed there is proof in the second dialogue that this is precisely what Mademoiselle is up to. As the conversation progresses, Mademoiselle and Bordeu become increasingly closer physically — at Mademoiselle's behest. At one point, for example, she says to him: "Doctor, come closer" (140). And she also uses the power of suggestion, having at an earlier point offered Bordeu a graphic illustration of the way two molecules that possess sensibility can fuse to become one.

> Here is an experiment I've performed a hundred times . . . but wait . . . I must go see what is happening behind those curtains. . . . When I place my hand on my thigh, at first I can feel distinctly that my hand is not my thigh, but some time later, once the amount of heat is equal in one and the other, I can no longer tell them apart; the boundaries of the two parts merge and [they] form only one. (134)

Mademoiselle's "experiment" is a fine example of the unity of form and content, for at the same time that she is discussing the union of molecules, she is preparing the way for another kind of union. The way she chooses to illustrate her point allows Mademoiselle to show off her thigh to Bordeu, an explicitly provocative act. Furthermore, by coyly peering behind the curtains to see if d'Alembert is awake before she uncovers herself, she makes the point that she is performing an intimate act intended for Bordeu's eyes only.

That Mademoiselle's tactics meet with some success is evident in Bordeu's reaction to a point Mademoiselle makes.

> BORDEU That's it. Come here so that I can kiss you.
> MADEMOISELLE Gladly. (148)

But the physical contact between Mademoiselle and Bordeu goes no further in the second dialogue. The most Mademoiselle is able to do is exact a promise from him that he will return to continue their conversation after he sees his next patient. By now, Mademoiselle obviously has a specific activity in mind for their next confrontation. Bordeu, nevertheless, is still in the dark about the implications of his return. Ironically, it is Bordeu himself who sums up the situation, without realizing that he is doing so, when in response to d'Alembert's question: "Doctor, do we understand each other? Are we understood?"

(192), he replies: "And for the mere reason that no one man perfectly resembles another, we never understand precisely, we are never precisely understood; there is always approximation in everything: our language always falls short of the sensation or goes beyond it" (193).

The differences between Bordeu, who is dominated by reason, and Mademoiselle, who is dominated by sensibility, have made Bordeu incapable of understanding that he has become the object of Mademoiselle de l'Espinasse's desire, that she has all along been using every strategy she can think of to seduce him. However, Bordeu will soon discover the truth in the course of the third dialogue, when he and Mademoiselle again take up the thread of their discussion.

At the beginning of the third dialogue, Mademoiselle finds herself "in a tête-à-tête" (195) with Bordeu, no longer encumbered by d'Alembert. It quickly becomes evident, moreover, that Mademoiselle and Bordeu have traded places, she having become the pursuer and he the pursued, for she is now the one who takes the lead in asking the questions. She immediately reopens the subject that had been left in suspension at the end of their previous encounter: "What do you think of the mingling of species?" (195). This question is not a disinterested one. Though it refers on one level to the arguments about generation and union among animal species that Bordeu had presented in their earlier exchange, on another level it refers to a more pointed mingling that Mademoiselle hopes will take place with Bordeu. But Bordeu, who is still unaware, proceeds to answer Mademoiselle's question exclusively on the intellectual level.

Even on this level, however, Mademoiselle's question leads Bordeu into ever more dangerous territory, since the subjects he must discuss to answer her query have to do with specifically sexual processes in nature. These subjects in turn launch Bordeu on a diatribe against the conventional morality of eighteenth-century society.

Mademoiselle nevertheless realizes that Bordeu is still missing the point. She therefore asks him the same question again: "But look here, Doctor, the most honest route and the quickest is to jump over the quagmire and come back to my first question: What do you think of the mingling of species?" (203) Bordeu naively answers: "We don't need to jump for that; we were already there. Is your question about physical science or morality?" (203) Mademoiselle can scarcely be more explicit than when she irritably answers: "About physical science, about physical science" (203). Undaunted, Bordeu continues the discussion in the same way as before. It is not until a little while later, in the middle of a discussion about the possibility of forming a new race by combining goats and men, that Bordeu suddenly realizes that he has fallen under Mademoiselle's spell and that she is in fact on the verge of successfully seducing him. This happens when Mademoiselle coyly asks Bordeu whether the new race of goat-men will be moral beings. The following exchange ensues:

> BORDEU I don't guarantee that they'll be very moral.
> MADEMOISELLE There will be no more safety for honest women; they will multiply endlessly; in the long run it will become necessary to destroy them or to obey them. I don't want any more of it, I don't want any more of it. Be still.   (206)

With this hysterical outburst of Mademoiselle's, which reveals that she has already imagined herself to be the unwilling victim of the goat-men's immorality, Bordeu begins to understand what has been happening all along. Up to now, he thought he was seducing Mademoiselle intellectually with conversation. Suddenly, however, he realizes that Mademoiselle has been using the same conversation to seduce him physically. It is at this point that the opposition he thought existed between reason and sensibility breaks down altogether. He finally understands—not just intellectually, as he had before, but also physically, having at last experienced the effects of Mademoiselle's tactics—that reason and sensibility are two sides of the same coin.

Although one might expect Bordeu to pursue the possibility of physical union with Mademoiselle once he understands the stakes, in fact what happens is just the opposite. The moment Bordeu understands that he has been a willing accomplice in his own seduction, he bids Mademoiselle good-bye.

Bordeu's sudden departure can be ascribed to a tactical error that Mademoiselle commits. As the second and third dialogues unfold, her strategies of seduction become increasingly obvious. Indeed, as we have seen, by the time the third dialogue begins to draw to a close, she is virtually stating her desires openly and directly to Bordeu. This approach accounts for Bordeu's decision to end the exchange with Mademoiselle, for once she stops using indirect tactics, the seduction becomes ineffective. Like Suzanne Simonin, then, Mademoiselle learns at the end of the third dialogue that once something has been stated directly, it is removed from the domain of action. Effective communication—or indeed effective seduction, which in this case is synonymous—requires an indirect approach.

But Mademoiselle's amorous defeat also serves another purpose. Throughout this discussion of the *Rêve*, we have seen how the acquisition of active sensibility is contagious. The *Rêve* begins in midstream; after Diderot has presumably caught sensibility from someone else, he then transmits it to d'Alembert, who transmits it to Mademoiselle, who in turn transmits it to Bordeu. And though the conversation between Bordeu and Mademoiselle breaks off and goes no further, the implicit assumption is that the next person that either interlocutor comes into contact with will also be contaminated with sensibility. Bordeu will go on to see another patient after he leaves Mademoiselle and transmit his condition either to that patient or to someone else, thus beginning the cycle all over again. Mademoiselle will also do the same, as she reveals in parting:

MADEMOISELLE Good-bye then, Doctor . . . if people knew all the horrors you have recounted to me.
BORDEU I am sure that you will keep quiet about them.
MADEMOISELLE Don't count on it, I only listen for the pleasure of retelling. (206)

With this statement, Mademoiselle makes it clear that the circuit of communication that has linked her to Bordeu throughout the second and third dialogues will now open up to other interlocutors. After Bordeu's departure, she will undoubtedly begin a conversation with someone else and, by so doing, once again activate the same process of communication/seduction.

But the circuit of communication does not just open up to other interlocutors in the fictional universe. In a move reminiscent of the ever-expanding circuit of communication in the *Préface-annexe* of *La Religieuse*, the opening of the third dialogue of the *Rêve de d'Alembert* poses the question of the reader.

There is evidence that Diderot had himself given serious thought to this question while he was composing the *Rêve de d'Alembert*. In a letter to Sophie Volland, Diderot describes the *Rêve de d'Alembert* and the reaction he would like a reader to have to this text:

> It is the most extreme extravagance and at the same time the most profound philosophy. There is some adroitness in having placed my ideas in the mouth of a man who is dreaming; it is often necessary to give wisdom an air of madness in order to find points of entry for it. I prefer that people say: "*But maybe that isn't as senseless as one might think,*" than that they say: "*Listen to me, those are very wise things.*"[20]

Diderot here distinguishes between a "bad" reader and a "good" one. The "bad" reader, who exclaims "Those are very wise things," is someone who probably already has intellectual affinities with the ideas that Diderot presents in the *Rêve* and therefore can maintain a cool though admiring distance from the text. Ultimately, however, he remains unaffected by it. The "good" reader, on the other hand, exclaims "That isn't as senseless as one might think," a reaction that shows that he has undergone a process resembling the one that the interlocutors in the *Rêve* undergo. His reaction implies that when first confronted with Diderot's hypotheses, he experienced the same initial incomprehension as did d'Alembert and Mademoiselle. Using only his intellectual faculties, he judged them to be senseless. But this is only his first reaction, for on second thought—and presumably after enough time has gone by to allow the physical and intellectual seduction operated by the text to take hold—the reader's point of view has been at least partially transformed, since he no longer thinks that Diderot's ideas are "*as* senseless" as he originally did.

To increase the chances that readers will have the latter reaction, Diderot distracts the reader's attention from the purely intellectual side of the issues being discussed among the various interlocutors by giving a prominent role in the second and third dialogues to Mademoiselle de l'Espinasse's seductive voice and person. Implicitly, Diderot hopes that the spectacle of Mademoiselle's provocative behavior will have the same effect on the reader that the spectacle of d'Alembert's sensibility had on Mademoiselle. But Diderot does not just rely on example to achieve his goal; in the *Rêve*, he also provides *structural* points of insertion for the reader. In the second dialogue, for example, there is a moment when Mademoiselle, who has been quoting d'Alembert's dream from her notes, murmurs something that Bordeu does not understand.

>MADEMOISELLE [Referring to the section of d'Alembert's dream that she has just read from her transcript] Doctor, do you understand any of that?
>BORDEU Perfectly well.
>MADEMOISELLE You are very lucky. . . . Perhaps my difficulty comes from a mistaken idea.

BORDEU Are you the one who's speaking?
MADEMOISELLE No, it's the dreamer. (117)

At the point where Mademoiselle once again begins to quote d'Alembert, the shift from direct discourse to indirect discourse is indicated by the suspension points that distinguish Mademoiselle's statement from d'Alembert's. But Bordeu, who is listening to Mademoiselle, does not have access to this typographical detail and therefore cannot distinguish her statement from the dreamer's. This ambiguity, however, does not exist for the reader, who sees the suspension points and can therefore distinguish Mademoiselle's statement from d'Alembert's. The conventions of writing thus privilege the reader's viewpoint over Bordeu's. This moment in the text involves the reader in the dynamic of exclusion and inclusion that characterizes the exchanges between the various interlocutors in the *Rêve*. Here the reader and Mademoiselle are included, and Bordeu is excluded; what is message for the reader and Mademoiselle is nothing but noise for Bordeu.

At another point in the second dialogue, a similar event takes place. Only this time the tables are turned, for it is Mademoiselle who is excluded and the reader and Bordeu who are included. This occurs when Bordeu whispers one of his speeches. Mademoiselle cannot hear what he has said, and inquires, "What are you muttering under your breath there, Doctor?" (126) Bordeu's full speech, however, appears in the text, thus granting the reader access to information unavailable to Mademoiselle. In this instance, what is noise for Mademoiselle is message for both the reader and Bordeu. The points of insertion in the *Rêve* thus establish strategic complicities with the reader, positioning the reader as an insider with respect to the textual universe, in much the same way as the *Préface-annexe* had.

We can now ask why Diderot goes to such lengths to tell the story of a physical and intellectual seduction that is ultimately designed to have the same effect on the reader. The answer to this question can be found in yet another trait of the *Rêve*. Although up to now I have insisted on the similarity that develops during the second dialogue in the interlocutors' modes of thinking, speaking, and acting, it now becomes necessary to make a finer distinction about the sorts of declarations and observations they make. What makes them similar to those originally made by Diderot in the first dialogue is their unorthodox philosophical perspective, which d'Alembert sums up when he declares: "Very well, here we have everything brought back to sensibility, memory, organic movements; that suits me rather well" (188). However, as the various interlocutors in the first and second dialogues take up the thread of Diderot's arguments, they do not reproduce them in exactly the same way. Although d'Alembert's statements as he dreams start out being virtually a repetition of those that Diderot had presented in the first dialogue, they subsequently take off in different directions. He departs from Diderot's argument about the mutability of the species and from it elaborates its cosmological implications, speculating on what life could be like on another planet, what species would evolve there, and so forth. Bordeu, whose arguments are essentially a continuation of Diderot's, tends nevertheless to emphasize their physiological implications. And in the third dialogue, Mademoiselle displaces the focus of the arguments about generation and union from the sphere of biology to that of morality.[21] Thus what we witness during the course of the second dialogue is a series of creative displacements of Diderot's ideas. By the end of the second dialogue they have undergone if not a complete transformation at least a redefinition of emphasis.

This aspect of the second dialogue is analogous to the third step in the biological processes traced in the first half of this chapter, namely, the creation of new entities, for we see the interlocutors beginning to steer the ideas they have assimilated in new directions. The third and final dialogue is especially important in this respect, both thematically and structurally. As Bordeu and Mademoiselle de l'Espinasse continue their discussion of generation and union, one of the subjects that they speculate about, as we saw earlier, is the formation of a race of goat-men, a race that would be altogether new: "[If men drank] goat's milk frequently . . . [if we trained] goats to feed on bread . . . we would derive from this a vigorous, intelligent, indefatigable and swift race" (205). The theme of the mingling of species is reflected in the structure of the exchange, as Bordeu and Mademoiselle, after excluding d'Alembert from their midst, have themselves formed a new alliance that could potentially make them the progenitors of a new race, should their union be consummated.

Again, what we see happening to the interlocutors provides clues to what is at stake in the process that Diderot would like the reader to undergo. Like generative processes in nature, the seduction the characters experience is generative both physically (in its most literal sense, since it can lead to sexual union and thus potentially to procreation) and intellectually (since the characters do not merely reproduce Diderot's arguments verbatim but produce new ones). If Diderot succeeds in his attempt to seduce the reader, if the "sounds" that his characters emit reach the reader's body and activate his sensibility, then the *Rêve* will have fulfilled its purpose. It will have served as a vehicle for persuading the reader of the viability of Diderot's materialist explanation of the workings of nature and, by so doing, will create the conditions that allow the reader to produce his own creative displacements of Diderot's ideas.

The *Rêve de d'Alembert* thus proposes a unique approach to persuasion. Whereas the goal of persuasive strategies is usually to change someone's mind about something, thus implying that the process has been completed once one person has passively assimilated another's ideas, the goal of Diderot's persuasive strategies is to encourage the reader to become active in the production of new ideas. Moreover, though it is generally assumed that persuasion is an intellectual process, in the *Rêve* it is defined as a material one. As we saw earlier, it is not the semantic content of the interlocutors' statements that produces change but rather the materiality of the statements—the sounds the interlocutors emit—that trigger a change in the other interlocutors' bodies and, by extension, minds. What the *Rêve* allows us to define, then, is a materialist rhetoric. This last point provides us with a vantage point from which to look back, reevaluate our trajectory, and draw conclusions.

CHAPTER SIX

CONCLUSION

Our reading of the *Rêve de d'Alembert* allows us to explain one of the recurrent features of Diderot's texts: the points of insertion for the reader that result from Diderot's use of a ternary model of communication. As we saw throughout the four preceding chapters, Diderot's model consistently opens out to the reader and draws him in as one of its terms.

In the *Préface-annexe* of *La Religieuse*, the "letter that was never sent" pulls the reader into the plot by making him a complicitous possessor of secret information available only to the conspirators. In the rest of *La Religieuse*, the most dramatic point of insertion for the reader appears in the scene that depicts the musical conversation between Suzanne and Ursule, during the course of which the reader not only is granted a privileged perspective on the exchange between the two nuns but also participates actively in the elaboration of part of the narrative structure. In the *Essai sur les règnes de Claude et de Néron*, Diderot repeatedly creates points of insertion for the reader by including him in imaginary conversations with historical personages and by instructing the reader to participate in the elaboration of the *Essai*'s intertext by reading Seneca along with Diderot. And in much the same way, the *Rêve de d'Alembert* provides points of insertion for the reader not only at the moments in the conversation among the various characters when the reader becomes privy to parts of the exchange to which other characters do not have access, but also at the end of the third dialogue, when the circuit of communication that had all along linked Mademoiselle, d'Alembert, Diderot, and Bordeu opens out to the reader.

Whereas in all these texts the points of insertion remain implicit, in *Jacques le fataliste* they are explicit. The narrator repeatedly invokes a hypostatized reader who becomes his fictive interlocutor, providing comments and objections about events and characters in the text. The narrator also includes the actual reader of *Jacques* in the fictional universe when he invites the reader to participate in the elaboration of the narrative by choosing from among several possible endings the one that he deems most appropriate.

Of the texts we have studied, however, it is the *Rêve de d'Alembert* that provides the key for understanding the reasons why points of insertion for the reader recur throughout Diderot's writings. These points of insertion are designed to establish a kind of physical contact between the textual universe and the reader, the same kind of contact that, as we saw throughout the *Rêve*, is invariably the initial step in generative processes. This is textual seduction in its most literal sense: Diderot's points of insertion constitute an attempt to put the body of the reader in a position that allows him to touch the "body" of the text. It is as if by attempting to establish contiguity between the reader and the characters and events in the textual universe, Diderot were trying to recreate for the reader the same conditions that made it possible in the *Rêve* for d'Alembert and Mademoiselle de l'Espinasse to move from a state of inert sensibility to a state of active sensibility, the crucial transformation that eventually allowed each of them to philosophize. Not only is Diderot's model of communication indirect, then, but it is designed to establish an indirect relationship with the reader. Its role, in other words, is to affect the reader's body as a way of indirectly affecting his mind.

This is also true of another recurrent feature in Diderot's texts: his representation of his characters' affective states. These scenes also seek to have an effect on the reader's body. Such a notion can make sense, however, only if we understand that for Diderot affective states are not psychological but physiological. As a result, when a narrator like Suzanne Simonin claims that her voice has a "touching sound," a trait that can be attributed not just to her singing voice but also to her narrating voice, her claim should be read literally. It is as if her voice were able to establish physical contact with her various audiences, and through this direct contact have an indirect effect on the affective state of listeners and readers alike.

When Suzanne achieves her goal, furthermore, when her voice touches her audience, it sets off a seemingly contagious process, in the course of which a character "catches" Suzanne's affect and then transmits it to another. As we saw earlier, the *Préface-annexe* of *La Religieuse* describes in detail the affective change in the conspirators as each comes into contact with Suzanne's narrative voice, first through her letters and then indirectly through "Madame Madin's," a process that results in the transformation of their laughter into tears. The rest of *La Religieuse* contains many other instances of contagious affective states, both negative and positive. Madame de Moni, for example, catches Suzanne's depression, and this eventually leads her to lose her talent for communicating with God. At those moments when Suzanne is absorbed in her singing or in prayer, the nuns who watch or listen are drawn to her and forget their previously negative judgments of her. Indeed their disapproval of Suzanne is transformed into sympathy and compassion. Thus the physical/affective change that takes place in the members of Suzanne's audience once they are touched and have caught her affect allows them to change their minds about her.

It is clear that the scenes in *La Religieuse* in which Diderot describes the affective states of his characters trace the same process we saw at work repeatedly in the *Rêve de d'Alembert*, in which messages take a detour through the body to reach the mind. This is a literary illustration of a notion that Diderot states explicitly in the *Eléments de physiologie*: the passions are states of the body that affect the mind. Furthermore, we can again speculate that these scenes fulfill a strategic function in relation to the reader. A reader who "enters" the textual universe through the points of insertion will come into contact with the fictional characters' affect and also catch it. That contact with the characters' affective states, particularly with Suzanne's, can indeed produce this transformation in the reader is evidenced by previous critical studies of *La Religieuse*, which claim that the affective charge of Suzanne's narration is so strong that in a first reading it allows the reader to overlook the work's logical inconsistencies. This is also true of the *Préface-annexe*; the contagion experienced by the conspirators seems to spread to its readers, who, following the example of the characters, get so carried away with the pathos of Suzanne's situation that they repeatedly lose their ability to distinguish fact from fiction.

A similar process is illustrated in the other texts we examined. In *Jacques le fataliste*, the constant interruption and postponement of the tales told by Jacques as well as the tales told by other narrators builds up a contagious sense of urgency to arrive at the end, an urgency that ends up being shared not just by the fictional characters but also by the reader of the novel. In the *Essai sur les règnes de Claude et de Néron*, Diderot urges the reader to read and reread Seneca, for only by doing so will the reader be able to develop the same kind of affective links that bind Diderot and his philosophical friends to the ancient Roman philosopher. His claim is that these affective links are necessary to the reader's ability to understand the arguments that Diderot presents in the *Essai*. And of course, contagious affective states abound in the *Rêve de d'Alembert*, the text in which Diderot both theorizes the principles of material communication and applies them not just to the relationship that develops among the characters in the text but also to the relationship that the *Rêve* engages with the reader.

In short, Diderot's recurrent use of points of insertion and his representation of contagious affective states are strategies of indirection, strategies that are aimed at creating the kind of physical contact with the reader that will eventually attain the reader's mind and provoke a series of productive transformations in his ways of thinking. This study shows that it is not just in the *Rêve de d'Alembert* but also in a variety of other texts that Diderot structures the relationship with the reader according to the materialist rhetoric he elaborates in the *Rêve*. It also brings into focus the ultimate case of Diderot's ternary model of communication. In this final instance, the third term that allows communication to take place between reader and text is not just another interlocutor but the body itself as interlocutor—and specifically the reader's body. For Diderot, as we have seen repeatedly throughout this study, messages travel not from one mind to another but from the body to the mind. Hence the necessity of a material analysis to understand that Diderot's communicational model is designed to bring into play not just the reader's mind but also the reader's body.

Thus the particular relationship that Diderot attempts to instigate between reader and text gives the reader access to a unique experience. In each of the instances we examined, we observed that the reader engages in an interactive relationship with Diderot's texts. Like the molecules Diderot describes in the *Rêve*, which act and react to each other, Diderot's texts do not merely act on the reader. Rather, they position him in such a way that he must interact with them. As we saw in the course of our analysis, not only does the reader at times take an active role in extending or completing parts of the narrative structure, but he also becomes an active participant in "conversations" with the figures who are portrayed in them. Rather than feeding the reader a content that can be consumed passively, then, the texts we have studied attempt to teach him to be an active practitioner of literature, history, and natural philosophy.

The *Préface-annexe* of *La Religieuse* makes the reader aware of his own susceptibility to the seductiveness of fiction, even as it unveils the mechanisms that create this effect—all the time making him an active participant in the very process that will result in his own seduction. The lessons of *La Religieuse* are reiterated in *Jacques le fataliste*, except that in this instance they are explicitly theorized by the "author"-narrator who constantly taunts the reader with his own power both to create and destroy illusions and thereby manipulate the reader's perceptions. In a different domain, the *Essai sur les règnes de Claude et de Néron*, rather than presenting the reader with historical facts that he can assimilate passively, takes the reader through an intricate process that teaches him to do the work of a Diderotian historian by interacting with texts, events, and personages both from the ancient Roman past and the Enlightenment present. Finally, the *Rêve de d'Alembert* prepares the reader not only to understand the workings of nature from a materialist perspective, but eventually to use this perspective to move natural philosophy in new directions.

What becomes increasingly clear is that in all the texts we studied, which are drawn from domains as diverse as fiction, history, and natural philosophy, Diderot places the emphasis not on content—the content that is supposed to determine the differences among these domains—but on process, on the process of creating fictional illusions, of reconstructing historical events, of interpreting nature from a materialist perspective. In each of these disparate domains, furthermore, the same process is at work. It is consistently the product of the materialist rhetoric that Diderot elaborates in the *Rêve de d'Alembert*, what in contemporary terms might be characterized as a "hands-on" interaction between reader and text.

I hope that my study has established a certain coherence for a corpus of texts that have often been accused of being incoherent and unsystematic. Our examination of texts from a variety of domains has allowed us to explore the ramifications of Diderot's use of the same structure within a multiplicity of settings. It is the consistent recurrence of the same mechanism in these different contexts that brings into focus an unexpected unity in what at first looks like a disparate corpus. Whether in the domain of fiction, history, or natural philosophy, Diderot repeatedly has recourse to his ternary model of communication. But this unity only emerges through a reading that attempts to come to terms with Diderot's own idiosyncratic model of communication. Models imported from other sources would not account for all of its unique features: that it is designed to create points of insertion for the reader; that what is ultimately at stake in this model is indirection; that it is a materialist model, designed to touch the reader's body as a way of indirectly touching his mind. To my knowledge, no other model of communication possesses these characteristics, and no other model would have allowed me to link together texts so apparently unlike each other. This study of Diderot thus argues in favor of textually specific reading, the very reading that Diderot's texts make it difficult to avoid.

APPENDIX

THE "PRÉFACE-ANNEXE"
OF "LA RELIGIEUSE"

PREFACE OF THE PRECEDING WORK,
TAKEN FROM THE
"CORRESPONDANCE LITTÉRAIRE"
OF M. GRIMM, YEAR 1760

That charming Marquis had left us at the beginning of the year 1759 to go to his estates in Normandy, near Caen. He had promised us that he would stay there only for the amount of time necessary to put his affairs in order, but his stay prolonged itself imperceptibly; he had gathered his children there; he was very fond of his parish priest; he had abandoned himself to a passion for gardening; and since an imagination as vivid as his required real or imaginary objects of attachment, he had suddenly immersed himself in a life of the most profound devotion. Despite that, he still loved us tenderly, but it is likely that we would never again have seen him in Paris if he hadn't lost his two sons one after the other. This event returned him to us about four years ago, after an absence of more than eight years. His religious fervor evaporated, as everything evaporates in Paris, and today he is more likable than ever.

Since his loss was infinitely painful to us, we deliberated in

1760, after having borne his absence for more than fifteen months, on the means of getting him to return to Paris. The author of the preceding Memoirs remembered that some time before the Marquis's departure, there had been much talk in society about the case of a young nun from Longchamp who had initiated a judicial appeal of the vows that she had been forced to take by her parents. This poor recluse had interested the Marquis to such an extent that without having seen her, without knowing her name, without even verifying the facts, he had gone to petition all the councillors of the Great Chamber of the Paris Parlement on her behalf. Despite this generous intercession, I do not know by what bad fortune Sister Simonin lost her trial, and her vows were judged to be valid.

Monsieur Diderot decided to bring this incident back to life and make it work to our advantage. He pretended that the nun in question had had the good fortune to escape from her convent, and as a consequence he wrote to Monsieur de Croismare in her name, asking for help and protection. We hadn't lost hope of seeing him come with all possible dispatch to the rescue of his nun, or, if he detected our villainy at first glance and our plot thus failed, we were sure to be left at the very least with ample material to joke about. This notorious imposture took an altogether different turn, as you will see in the correspondence that I shall place before your eyes, which took place between Monsieur Diderot, or the would-be nun, and the loyal and charming Marquis de Croismare, who never suspected for an instant a perfidy that we had on our consciences for a long time. Back then we spent our suppers, amidst gales of laughter, reading letters that were supposed to make our good Marquis weep, and we also read with the same gales of laughter the sincere replies of our worthy and generous friend. Nevertheless, as soon as we realized that the fate of our unfortunate nun was beginning to interest her tender benefactor a little too much, Monsieur Diderot decided to have her put to death, preferring to cause the Marquis some grief than to take the obvious risk of tormenting him perhaps more cruelly by letting her live longer. After his return to Paris, we confessed our iniquitous plot to him; he laughed about it, as you can well imagine, and the sufferings of the poor nun served only to strengthen the ties of friendship among those who survived her—yet he never spoke about the plot with Monsieur Diderot. One incident, and not the least singular, is that while this mystification was kindling the imagination of our friend in Normandy, it was also kindling Diderot's. The latter, who was convinced that the Marquis would not offer shelter in his house to a young woman whom he did not know, began to write in detail the story of our nun. One day when he was engrossed in this work, M. d'Alainville, one of our mutual friends, came to visit, and found him engulfed in sorrow, his face streaming with tears. "What is wrong?" d'Alainville asked him. "What a state you're in!" "What is wrong," M. Diderot answered, "is that I am deeply grieved by a story I am inventing." It is certain that if he'd finished this tale, it would have become one of our truest, most interesting, and most pathos-laden novels. You couldn't read a single page of it without shedding tears, and yet there was no love story. It was a work of genius that everywhere bore the distinctive stamp of the author's imagination and a work of general and public utility, since it was the cruelest satire that had ever been written about convents. It was all the more dangerous because the first part was full of praise for them; the young nun had the devoutness of an angel and nurtured in her simple and tender heart the most sincere respect for everything she had been taught to hold in esteem. But this novel existed only in fragments and never went beyond that state; it has been lost, like an infinity of other works written by an exceptional man, who would have been immortalized by twenty masterpieces if only he had put his time to better use and had not given it away to a thousand heedless individuals, all of whom I call to the Last Judgment, where they will answer before God and before men to the crime of which they are guilty.

(And I myself, who know M. Diderot a little, will add that he in fact completed this novel, which is none other than the very Memoirs you have just read, and in which you must have noticed how important it is not to trust the praise of friends.)

This correspondence and our repentance are therefore all that remain of our poor nun. Please remember that the letters signed Madin, or Suzanne Simonin, were fabricated by that child of Belial, and that the letters of the nun's generous protector are authentic and were written in good faith, though we had an enormously difficult time persuading M. Diderot of this, since he firmly believed that the Marquis and his own friends were playing a joke on him.

NOTE FROM THE NUN TO M. THE COMTE DE CROISMARE, GOVERNOR OF THE ROYAL MILITARY SCHOOL

An unhappy woman in whom Monsieur the Marquis de Croismare took an interest three years ago, when he lived next to the Academy of Music, has learned that he currently resides at the Military School. She asks to know if she can still count on his kindness, now that she is more to be pitied than ever.

A word in return, if it so pleases him. Her situation is pressing, and it is of great consequence that the person who will hand him this note suspect nothing.

She was told that there had been a mistake, and that the Monsieur de Croismare in question was currently living in Caen.

This note had been written in the hand of a young woman whose services we employed throughout the course of this correspondence. A pageboy from the neighborhood took the message to the Military School and brought back the reply. M. Diderot thought that this first step was necessary for several good reasons. It made the nun appear to be confusing the two cousins and not to know the true spelling of their name; in this way she learned quite naturally that her protector was living in Caen. There also existed the possibility that the governor of the Royal Military School would tease his cousin about the note and send it to him, which would give an air of great authenticity to our virtuous adventurer. This Governor, who was very likable, as is everything that carries his name, was just as weary of his cousin's absence as we were, and we hoped to include him in the ranks of the conspirators. After his reply, the nun wrote to Caen.

LETTER
FROM THE NUN TO M. THE MARQUIS
DE CROISMARE IN CAEN

Monsieur, I do not know to whom I am writing, but in my present distress, whoever you may be, it is to you that I turn. If I have not been misinformed at the Military School and if you are indeed the generous Marquis whom I seek, I shall thank God; if you are not, I do not know what I shall do. But the name you bear reassures me; I hope that you will come to the rescue of an unfortunate young woman on whose behalf you, Monsieur, or another Monsieur de Croismare who is not the one from the Military School, used your influence in an unsuccessful attempt she made two years ago to leave a perpetual prison to which she had been condemned by her parents' severity. Despair has driven me to take a second step in this direction, a step about which you have no doubt heard: I have escaped from my convent. I could no longer endure what I had to suffer there, and there was only this avenue open to me, or else a far more serious crime, to gain the freedom I had sought from the fairness of the law.

Monsieur, if you are my former protector, may my current

situation touch your heart and reawake in you a feeling of pity! Perhaps you will find it imprudent of me to have recourse to a stranger in circumstances like mine. Alas, Monsieur, if you knew the forlorn state to which I have been reduced, if you had any idea of the inhumanity with which scandals are punished in religious houses, you would excuse me. But you have a sensitive soul, and you will fear having one day to remember an innocent creature thrown for the rest of her life into a dark cell. Help me, Monsieur, help me, it will be a good deed that you will remember with satisfaction as long as you live, and that God will reward in this life or in the next. Most of all, Monsieur, keep in mind that I live in perpetual fear and that I'll be counting the moments until I hear from you. The members of my family must suspect that I am in Paris; they are surely making all sorts of inquiries in order to discover my whereabouts; do not give them the time to find me. Up to now I have survived by means of my work and the kindness of a worthy woman who was my friend, and to whom you can address your reply. Her name is Madame Madin and she lives in Versailles. This good friend will provide me with everything I shall need for the journey, and once placed, I shall need nothing more and will no longer be dependent on her. Monsieur, my conduct will justify the protection that you may accord me. Whatever your reply, I shall blame only my unhappy fate.

Here is Madame Madin's address: *Madame Madin, Pavillon de Bourgogne, rue d'Anjou, Versailles.*

Please be good enough to use two envelopes, with her address on the first, and a cross on the second.

Dear God, I do so long to have your answer! I am continually in fear.

Your most humble and obedient servant.

— Signed, Suzanne Simonin

A longer version of this letter can be found at the end of the novel, where M. Diderot inserted it when, having neglected this formless sketch for twenty-one years, it fell into his hands again and he determined to touch it up.

We needed an address to receive the replies, and so we chose a certain Madame Madin, wife of a former infantry officer, who really lived in Versailles. She knew nothing of our mischievousness, nor of the letters that we subsequently made her write, and for which we used the writing of another young woman. Madame Madin had merely been warned that she would have to receive and then forward to me all the letters postmarked *Caen*. As chance would have it, Monsieur de Croismare, after his return to Paris and approximately eight years after our sin, ran into Madame Madin one morning at the house of one of our women friends who had participated in the plot. It was a real *coup de théâtre*: Monsieur de Croismare had been intending to make a thousand inquiries about the unfortunate young woman who had so greatly interested him, and about whose existence Madame Madin knew nothing at all. This was also the moment for our general confession and absolution.

REPLY
FROM M. THE MARQUIS DE CROISMARE

Mademoiselle, your letter reached the very person you have been seeking. You were not mistaken about his feelings, and you can leave immediately for Caen, if a place at the side of a young lady suits you.

Have the lady who is your friend write me a letter stating that she is sending me a lady's maid of the kind I require, with whatever praises of your qualities as she may want to include, and without going into detail about your situation. Have her indicate also the name you will have chosen, the carriage in which you will arrive, and if possible, the day of your departure. If you were to take the Caen coach, you would board it very early Monday morning and arrive here Friday; it is stabled at the Grand Cerf, rue St. Denis, in Paris. If it so happens that there is no one to meet you when you arrive in Caen, you can, in the meantime, address yourself as coming from me to Monsieur Gassion, who lives opposite the Place Royale. Since it is of the utmost importance on your part and mine that we remain incognito, have your friend send me back this letter, in which you can have complete faith, although it is unsigned. Save only the seal, which will allow you to identify yourself to the person to whom you will address yourself.

Follow precisely and diligently the stipulations in this letter, Mademoiselle; and, for the sake of prudence, do not carry with you any papers, letters, or any other thing that might give away your identity; it will be easy to send for all those things at a later time. You can count with full confidence on the good intentions of your servant.

From . . . near Caen, on this Wednesday, 6 February 1760

This letter was addressed to Madame Madin. On the other envelope there was a cross, according to the agreement. The seal represented a cupid holding a torch in one hand and two hearts in the other, with a motto that we were unable to read, because the seal had been damaged when the letter was opened. It was natural that a young nun who knew nothing about love should take the image for that of her guardian angel.

REPLY
FROM THE NUN TO
M. THE MARQUIS DE CROISMARE

Monsieur, I received your letter. I think that I have been ill, very ill. I am very weak. If God calls me to him, I shall pray ceaselessly for your salvation; if I recover from this illness, I shall do everything that you order. My dear Sir! Honorable man! I shall never forget your kindness.

My worthy friend should be arriving any moment from Versailles; she will tell you everything.

On this holy Sunday in February I shall keep the seal carefully. There is a holy angel stamped on it; it is you, it is my guardian angel.

Since M. Diderot had been unable to attend the bandits' meeting, this reply had been sent without his approval. It was not to his liking; he maintained that it would expose our treachery. He was mistaken, and he was wrong, I think, to dislike this reply. Nevertheless, to satisfy him we set down in the register of the proceedings of our imposture the answer that follows and that was never sent. This illness, moreover, was indispensable in order to delay the departure for Caen.

EXCERPT FROM THE REGISTER

The preceding letter was the one that was sent, and here is the one that Sister Suzanne should have written:

Monsieur, I thank you for all your kindness. I should no longer plan on anything; everything will end for me; I shall very shortly be before the God of mercy; it is there that I shall remember you. They are debating whether or not to bleed me for a third time; they will order whatever they please. Goodbye, my dear Sir. I hope that the place where I am going will be happier; we shall see each other there.

LETTER
FROM MADAME MADIN
TO M. THE MARQUIS DE CROISMARE

I am at her bedside, and she urges me to write to you. She has been in the utmost extremity, and my station, which keeps me tied to Versailles, did not allow me to come to her aid any sooner. I knew that she was very ill and had been abandoned by everyone, but I could not leave. You can well imagine, Monsieur, how much she suffered. She had fallen and had been hiding the fall. She was consumed all of a sudden by a burning fever that could only be lowered through bleedings. I believe her to be out of danger now. What troubles me at present is the fear that her convalescence may be long and that she will be unable to leave for another month or six weeks; she is already so weak and will be even more so with time. Try therefore, Monsieur, to gain some time, and let us work together to save the most unfortunate and most interesting creature in the world. I cannot describe the full impact of your letter on her; she wept a great deal, she wrote M. Gassion's address on the back of a plate of Saint Suzanne in her prayerbook, and afterwards she wrote to you in spite of her weakness. She had just come through a crisis, and I do not know what she could have told you, for she barely had her poor wits about her. Pardon me, Monsieur, I am writing you in haste. I feel sorry for her; I do not want to leave her, but it is impossible for me to stay here for several days in a row. I am enclosing the letter that you wrote her; I am sending along with it another one more or less of the kind you requested. In it I do not mention any of her pleasing skills, since they will have nothing to do with the position she is about to take on, and it is necessary, in my opinion, for her to give them up if she wants to remain unnoticed. Moreover, everything I am telling you about her is true; indeed, Monsieur, there is no mother on earth who would not be gratified to the fullest to have her for a daughter. My first concern, as you can imagine, was to hide her away, and this I have done. I shall agree to let her leave only after she has fully recovered her health, but this will take at least a month or six weeks, as I had the honor of telling you earlier, and even then only if there are no intervening accidents. She is keeping the seal from your letter; it is in her book of Hours under her pillow. I didn't dare tell her that it wasn't yours; I had broken it when I opened your letter and replaced it with mine. Given the sorry state she's in, I couldn't risk giving her your letter without reading it first. I dare to ask you on her behalf for a note that will keep up her hopes; they are all she has left, and I fear for her life if she were to lose them. If you would be kind enough to send me a separate description of the house she will be entering, I shall use it to reassure her. Have no fears about your letters, they will all be sent back to you as punctually as the first; you can put your trust in the stake that I myself have in not doing anything rash. We shall comply with everything, unless your intentions change. Goodbye, Monsieur. Our dear unfortunate child prays for you whenever the state of her mind allows.

I wait for your answer, Monsieur, still at the Pavillon de Bourgogne, rue d'Anjou, Versailles.

On this 16 February 1760

OPEN LETTER
FROM MADAME MADIN,
AS REQUESTED BY M. THE MARQUIS DE CROISMARE

Monsieur, the person I am recommending is named Suzanne Simonin. I love her as if she were my own daughter; nevertheless, you can take everything I shall tell you about her to the letter, because it is not in my nature to exaggerate. She has lost both her father and her mother; she comes from a good family and her education has not been neglected. She is skilled in all the various kinds of fancy needlework that you learn when you are dexterous and like to keep busy. She speaks little, but expresses herself fairly well; she writes with ease. If the person for whom you intend her would like to be read to, she reads marvelously well. She is neither tall nor short; she is shapely; as for her physiognomy, I have seldom seen a more interesting one. You will find her perhaps a bit young, as I think she is barely seventeen years old, but if she lacks the experience that comes with age, she makes up for it with the experience that comes with suffering. She is circumspect and has unusually good judgment. I can answer for the innocence of her morals. She is pious, but not at all narrow-minded. She is naive, full of gentle gaiety, never in a bad mood. I have two daughters; if certain circumstances didn't prevent Mademoiselle Simonin from settling in Paris, I would not have to look elsewhere to find a governess for them, as I have no hope of discovering anyone better. I have known her since she was a child, and she has always lived under my watchful eye. She will be fitted out well when she leaves here. I shall take care of whatever small expenses her journey may incur, and even those of her return, should you send her back to me; it is the least I can do for her. She has never been outside Paris, she has no idea where she is going, she thinks she's done for, and I have a great deal of difficulty in calming her fears. A word from you, Monsieur, about the person whom she will serve, the house where she will live, and the duties that she will have to fulfill, will do more for her state of mind than all my speeches. Would it be demanding too much of your goodwill to ask you to comply with this request? Her one fear is that she will not meet with success; the poor child does not know her own worth.

    I have the honor of being, with all the consideration that you deserve, Monsieur, your most humble and obedient servant.

—Signed, Moreau Madin
Paris, on this 16 February 1760

LETTER
FROM M. THE MARQUIS DE CROISMARE
TO MADAME MADIN

Madame, two days ago I received a brief note informing me of Mademoiselle Simonin's indisposition. I lament her unhappy fate; her health worries me. May I ask of you the consolation of keeping me informed about her condition, about the steps she plans to take—in short, to answer the letter I wrote her? I dare to hope from your good nature and your own interest in these matters that you will comply with this request.

Your very humble and obedient, etc.

Caen, on this 19 February 1760

ANOTHER LETTER
FROM M. THE MARQUIS DE CROISMARE TO
MADAME MADIN

I was most impatient, Madame, and fortunately your letter put an end to my worries about Mademoiselle Simonin, who, as you assure me, is out of danger and safe from being found out. I am writing to her, and you can reassure her again about my continuing concern for her. Her letter made a strong impression on me, and given the difficulties in which I saw her, I thought I could do no better than to place her in service to my daughter, who unfortunately no longer has a mother. This is the house I have in mind for her, Madame. I have confidence in myself and in my ability to allay her suffering without giving away the secret, a task that in other hands would perhaps be more difficult. I will not be able to keep myself from lamenting both her current state and the state of my finances, which will not allow me to act toward her as I would wish, but what can one do when one is subject to the laws of necessity? I live two leagues away from the city in a rather pleasant part of the country, where I lead a very sheltered existence with my daughter and my eldest son, a young man who is very religious and full of good intentions, but who, nevertheless, will be kept in the dark about everything that concerns her. As for the servants, they are people who have been in my service for a long time, so that everything here is very calm and harmonious. I would like to add, furthermore, that the course of action I am offering her need only be her last resort. If she finds something better, I have no intention of holding her to a contract, but let her be certain that she will always find in me a steady source of support. May she therefore recover her health without having to worry; I shall wait for her, and meanwhile will be very glad to have frequent news of her.

I have the honor of being, Madame, etc.

Caen, on this 21 February 1760

LETTER FROM M. THE MARQUIS DE CROISMARE TO SISTER SUZANNE

(There was a cross on the envelope.)

Mademoiselle, no one can be more deeply affected than I by the situation in which you find yourself. My concern to find you some consolation for the unhappy fate that pursues you has done nothing but increase. Calm yourself, regain your strength, and with full confidence count always on my concern for you. Nothing should occupy your mind except the recovery of your health and the care you must take to remain undiscovered. If it were possible for me to make your fate more bearable, I would do so; but I am hampered by your situation, and can only lament this harsh necessity. The person for whom I intend you is very dear to me, and you will answer principally to me; I shall thus take care, insofar as possible, to ease the small burdens of the position that you will be taking. You will owe me your confidence; I shall depend entirely on your efforts; this assurance should make you feel calmer and offer proof of my way of thinking and of the sincere attachment with which I remain, Mademoiselle, your etc.

Caen, on this 21 February 1760
I shall write to Madame Madin, who will be able to tell you more.

LETTER
FROM MADAME MADIN TO
M. THE MARQUIS DE CROISMARE

Monsieur, the recovery of our dear patient is now certain; no more fever, no more headaches; everything points to a quick convalescence and the best of health. Her lips are still a little pale, but her eyes are sparkling again; she is beginning to have color in her cheeks; her complexion is fresh and she will soon fill out again; everything is going well now that her mind is at peace. It is especially now, Monsieur, that she appreciates the value of your kindness, and nothing is more touching than the way in which she expresses it. I wish I could describe what passed between the two of us when I brought her your last letters. She took them; her hands were trembling; she barely breathed as she read them, stopping at every line; and, after she had finished, she said to me, throwing her arms around my neck and weeping profusely: "Well, Mama Madin, God has not abandoned me then, he wants me to be happy at last! Yes, it was God who inspired me to seek out that dear gentleman; who else in the world would have taken pity on me? Let us thank Heaven for these first favors, so that it will grant us more...."
And then she sat down on her bed and began to pray; afterwards, going back to certain passages in your letters, she said: "He is entrusting his daughter to me! Oh, Mama, she will no doubt look like him, she will be gentle, kind and sensitive like

him. . . . " After stopping herself, she said with some concern: "She no longer has a mother! I am sorry that I don't have the experience I need. I don't know anything but I shall do my best; I shall remind myself day and night of all that I owe her father; gratitude must surely make up for many things. Will I be sick for a long time still? When will they permit me to eat? I no longer feel anything from the fall, nothing at all." I am telling you these small details, Monsieur, because I hope they will please you. There was so much innocence and enthusiasm in her speech and her demeanor that I was profoundly moved myself. I would have given anything to have you see and hear her. No, Monsieur, either I have no judgment at all, or you have found a unique creature who will be the blessing of your household. Everything that you were good enough to tell me about yourself, your daughter, your son, and your circumstances, accords perfectly with her wishes. She abides by the terms she first proposed: she asks only for food and clothing, and you can take her at her word, if that suits you; even though I am not rich, I shall take care of the rest. I love this child, I have adopted her in my heart, and the little that I will have done for her during my lifetime will be continued after my death. I will not conceal from you that those words *her last resort* and *leaving her free to accept a better offer, if the opportunity presents itself*, wounded her; I was not displeased to discover this delicacy of feeling in her. I shall not neglect to keep you informed about the progress of her convalescence; but I have an ambitious project which I hope to carry out while she is recovering, if you could put me in touch with one of your friends, of which you no doubt have many here. It would require a wise, discreet, skillful, not too prominent man, who himself or through his friends could approach several Important Persons whose names I could provide, and who would have access to the Court without belonging to it. As I've arranged things in my mind, he would not be in on the secret and would serve us without knowing how.

Even if my plan is fruitless, we would benefit from it at least by creating the impression that she is in a foreign country. If you are able to put me in touch with someone, I beg you to tell me his name and his place of residence, and then to write him that Madame Madin, whom you have known for a long time, will be coming to ask him a favor and that you beg him to take an interest in her project, if it is feasible. If you have no one, we shall have to give up, but see what you can do, Monsieur. Moreover, I beg you to rely on the interest I take in our unfortunate friend and on whatever prudence I may have gained from experience. The joy caused by your last letter made her pulse skip, but it is nothing serious.

I have the honor of being, with the most respectful sentiments, Monsieur, your etc.

—Signed, Moreau Madin
Paris, on this 3 March 1760

Madame Madin's idea of approaching one of the generous protector's friends had been one of Satan's suggestions, by means of which his fellow demons hoped skillfully to inspire their friend in Normandy to address himself to me and to let me in on the secret of the whole affair, all of which succeeded perfectly, as you will see in the rest of this correspondence.

LETTER
FROM SISTER SUZANNE
TO M. THE MARQUIS DE CROISMARE

Monsieur, Mama Madin has given me the two replies with which you have honored me, and also informed me about the letter you had written her. I accept, I accept. It is a hundred times better than I deserve, yes a hundred times, a thousand times better. I have seen so little of society, I have so little experience, and I am so well aware of everything I would need to be worthy of the confidence you have in me; but I place all my hope in your indulgence, my zeal, and my gratitude. My position will shape me, and Mama Madin says that is better than if I had been shaped for the position. Dear God, I am in such a hurry to recover, to go and throw myself at the feet of my benefactor, and to serve him by serving his daughter in every way I can! I am told that this will take about a month; a month! that is a long time. My dear Sir, please continue to look on me with benevolence. I am beside myself with joy, but they do not want me to write, they prevent me from reading, they keep me in bed, they drown me in infusions, they starve me to death, and all of that for my own good. May God be praised! Nevertheless, in spite of myself I obey them.

I am, Monsieur, with a grateful heart, your very humble and submissive servant.

—Signed, Suzanne Simonin
Paris, on this 3 March 1760

LETTER
FROM M. THE MARQUIS DE CROISMARE
TO MADAME MADIN

Several indispositions from which I have been suffering for the past few days have prevented me, Madame, from answering you any sooner, and from indicating to you the pleasure I have to learn of Mademoiselle Simonin's convalescence. I dare to hope that in the very near future you will have the goodness to inform me of her complete recovery, for which I fervently hope. But I am mortified that I am unable to contribute to the execution of the project you are contemplating on her behalf; without knowing more about it, I can only judge its worth by the prudence of which you are capable and by the interest that you take in it. I have circulated very little in Paris, and only among a small number of persons who circulate as little as I, and acquaintances of the kind you desire are not easy to find. I beg you to continue sending me news of Mademoiselle Simonin, whose best interests will always be dear to me.

I have the honor of being, etc.

On this 13 March 1760

REPLY
FROM MADAME MADIN
TO M. THE MARQUIS DE CROISMARE

Monsieur, perhaps I was mistaken not to explain my project, but I was in such a hurry to move ahead with it! This then is what I had in mind. First, you must know that Cardinal *** protected the family. They all suffered a great loss when he died, especially my Suzanne, who had been presented to him as a very young child. The old Cardinal liked pretty children: the charms of this one had made an impression on him, and he had made himself responsible for her well-being; but when he died, they disposed of her as you well know, and the protectors thought they had lived up to their obligations to the youngest daughter by marrying off her elders. I therefore thought that if we could somehow approach the Marquise de T***, who is said to be if not compassionate, at least very active (but what does it matter through whom good deeds are done), and who did her utmost during my child's trial, and if we could portray the sad situation of a young woman exposed to all the consequences of poverty, in a faraway foreign land, we might in this way extract a small income from the two brothers-in-law who took all of the family's possessions, and who have no intention of helping us. In truth, Monsieur, it is well worth our while to reconsider this matter again; you see, with this small income, with what I have secured for her, and with whatever she might obtain from your generosity, she would be well provided for in the present, and not badly provided for in the future, and I would be less reluctant to see her leave. But I do not know Madame the Marquise de T***, nor the Secretary of the defunct Cardinal who is said to be a man of letters, nor anyone close to him, and it was the child who suggested that I ask you. For the rest I am unable to tell you that her convalescence is progressing as I would wish. She had injured her side, as I think I told you; the pain of this fall, which had vanished, has now reappeared; it comes and goes and is accompanied by a slight internal throbbing, but her pulse shows no signs of fever. The doctor shakes his head and has an expression that does not please me. Next Sunday she will go to Mass; she insists, and I have just sent her a coat with a hood that will cover her to the tip of her nose and under which I think she will be able to spend half an hour in a small obscure neighborhood church without running any risks. She longs for the moment of her departure, and I am sure that she will pray to God for her complete recovery and for the continued generosity of her benefactor with greater fervor than she will pray for anything else. If she were able to leave between Easter and the following Sunday, I would be sure to let you know. Besides, Monsieur, her absence would not prevent me from taking action if I were to find someone among my acquaintances who could have some influence on Madame de T*** and Doctor A***, who has a great deal of sway over her.

I am, Monsieur, with boundless gratitude on her part and mine, your most humble, etc.

—Signed, Moreau Madin
Versailles, on this 25 March 1760

P.S. I have forbidden her to write you for fear of importuning you; this is the only consideration that can prevent her from doing so.

REPLY FROM M. THE MARQUIS DE CROISMARE TO MADAME MADIN

Madame, your project for Mademoiselle Simonin seems very praiseworthy to me and pleases me all the more as I would fervently like to see her, in spite of her misfortune, assured of a tolerable situation. I do not despair of finding a friend who might have some influence with Madame de T***, or Doctor A***, or the Secretary of the late Cardinal, but this requires time and many precautions, as much to avoid revealing the secret as to assure myself of the discretion of the persons whom I think I could approach. I will not lose sight of that. In the meantime, if Mademoiselle Simonin continues in the same intentions, and if her health has improved sufficiently, nothing should keep her from leaving; she will find that the feelings I have already shown toward her have not changed and that I am still just as eager to assuage, if possible, the hardships of her fate. The state of my affairs and the difficulties of the times force me to lead a very retired life in the country with my children, for reasons of economy, and so we live very simply here. This is why Mademoiselle Simonin will not have to spend large sums for any particularly elegant or expensive clothing; ordinary ones will be sufficient here. It is in this part of the countryside and in this quiet and simple condition that she will find me, and it is here where I hope she will be able to find some pleasure and some enjoyment, despite the annoying precautions that I shall be forced to take with regard to her. Please have the goodness, Madame, to inform me of her departure, and for fear that she may have lost the address I sent her, it is M. Gassion's residence, across from the Place Royale in Caen. Nevertheless, if I am instructed in time about the day of her arrival, she will find someone waiting to bring her here directly.

I have the honor, Madame, of being your very humble, etc.

On this 31 March 1760

LETTER
FROM MADAME MADIN
TO M. THE MARQUIS DE CROISMARE

If she continues in the same intentions, Monsieur! How can you doubt it? Does she have anything better to do than to spend many happy and tranquil days in the presence of an upstanding man and a good family? Is she not overjoyed that you remembered her? And where would she lay her head if she lacked the shelter that you have had the generosity to provide her? She herself is the one, Monsieur, who speaks in this manner, and I am only repeating to you what she says. She still wanted to go to Mass on Easter; I was against it and it turned out badly: she returned with a fever, and since that unhappy day she has not been well. Monsieur, I shall not send her to you until she is in good health again. At present she has a burning sensation on her side, where she injured herself in the fall; I have just looked at it, and see nothing at all. But the day before yesterday, her doctor told me, as we were coming downstairs together, that he feared there might be the beginnings of a pulsation and that we had to wait to see how it would develop. Nevertheless she has not lost her appetite, she sleeps well and is still plump; it is only from time to time that I find she has a little more color in her cheeks and more sparkle in her eyes than she normally does. And furthermore her fits of impatience drive me to despair. She gets up, she tries to walk, but if she bends in the slightest toward the injured side, she lets out a sharp cry that pierces the heart. Despite this I have not lost hope, and I have taken advantage of the extra time to arrange her little wardrobe.

A dress of English calamanco, which she can wear without anything else until the summer heat subsides, and which she can later line for winter with another dress, of blue cotton, that she is wearing at present.

Fifteen camisoles, some made of cambric, the others of muslin. Around the middle of June I shall send her material with which to make six others out of a piece of linen that is being bleached for me in Senlis.

Several white petticoats, two of which I gave her, made of dimity and trimmed with muslin.

Two identical bodices that I had had made for my younger daughter and that turned out to fit Suzanne perfectly. This will give her something to wear for the summer.

Some corsets, aprons and neckerchiefs.

Two dozen pocket handkerchiefs.

Several nightcaps.

Six scalloped caps for day, along with eight pairs of cuffs with one ruffle, and three with two.

Six pairs of fine cotton stockings. This was the best I could do. I took these things to her the day after the holidays and I cannot tell you with how much emotion she accepted them. She would look at one thing, try on another, take my hands and kiss them. But she was unable to hold back her tears when she saw my daughter's bodices. "So?" I said to her, "why are you weeping? Haven't you always been like a daughter to me?" "It is true," she answered . . . and then she added: "Now that I hope to be happy, it seems to me that I would be sorry to die. Mama, isn't the burning in my side going to disappear? Couldn't we put something on it? . . . " I am delighted, Monsieur, that you do not disapprove of my plan, and that you see the possibility of having it succeed. I leave everything to your good judgment; but I think I should warn you that Madame the Marquise of T*** is leaving for the country, that Monsieur A*** is hard to reach and bad-tempered, that the Secretary, who is very proud of the title of academician he has finally obtained after twenty years of solicitations, is going back to Brittany, and that three or four months from now they will have forgotten us. Everything loses its interest so quickly in this country! People hardly speak about us any more, and soon they will not speak about us at all. Have no fear that she will lose the address you sent her. She never opens her book of Hours without looking at it; she is more likely to forget her own name of Simonin than that of M. Gassion. I asked her if she wanted to write you; she told me that she had started a long letter that would contain everything that she will not be able to refrain from telling you, if God grants her the favor of restoring her health and allowing her to see you, but that she had a presentiment that this would never happen. "This is taking too long, Mama," she added; "I won't benefit from his kindness or yours: either Monsieur the Marquis will change his mind, or I will not recover." "What foolishness!" I told her. "Don't you know that if you entertain these mournful thoughts what you fear will happen?" She said: "Let God's will be done" . . . I begged her to show me what she had written, and it frightened me. It is a book, a thick book. "This," I said to her angrily, "is precisely what is killing you." She answered: "What do you want me to do? Either I grieve or I am bored." "And when did you have the time to scribble all of that?" "A little at one time, a little at another. Whether I live or die, I want people to know what I have suffered" . . . I forbade her to continue; her doctor did also. I beg you, Monsieur, to add your authority to my entreaties, for she considers you her dear master and will certainly obey you. However, since I agree that the hours pass by very slowly for her and can see that she needs to stay occupied, even if only to prevent her from writing any more, from dreaming or from fretting, I brought her an embroidery frame and suggested that she begin a waistcoat for you. This idea pleased her enormously, and she began to work right away. May God will that she not have the time to finish it here! A word, if you please, forbidding her to write and to work too much. I had resolved to return to Versailles this evening, but I am anxious. This incipient pulsation worries me, and I want to be near her tomorrow when her doctor returns. Unfortunately I have some faith in the presentiments of people who are ill; they can sense what is happening to them. When I lost Monsieur Madin, all the doctors assured me that he would recover; he himself said that he would not, and the poor man's pronouncement turned out to be only too true. I shall stay here, and have the honor of writing to you. If I were to lose her, I do not think I would ever get over it. You, Monsieur, will have been only too lucky not to have seen her. It is only now that the wretched nuns who made her determine to escape are feeling the loss they have suffered, but it is too late.

I have the honor of being, Monsieur, with feelings of respect and gratitude both on her behalf and mine, your very humble, etc.

—Signed, Moreau Madin
Paris, on this 13 April 1760

REPLY
FROM M. THE MARQUIS DE CROISMARE
TO MADAME MADIN

I share, Madame, with real sympathy your anxiety about Mademoiselle Simonin's illness. Her unfortunate state had always infinitely touched me, but the details you were kind enough to give me of her qualities and feelings make me so partial to her that it would be impossible for me not to take the most serious interest in her. Thus, far from changing my feelings about her, I beg you to repeat to her those that I have expressed to you in my letters and which are not subject to alteration. I thought it prudent to refrain from writing to her, in order to avoid giving her the opportunity to reply. There can be no doubt that activities of any kind are harmful to her in her weak condition, and if I had some power over her, I would use it to forbid her from taking part in any. I can do no better than to ask you yourself, Madame, to let her know my opinions on this matter. It is not that I wouldn't be delighted to receive news from her personally, but I could not approve of an action that she might take out of sheer propriety, but which could contribute to delaying her recovery. The interest that you take in her, Madame, dispenses me from begging you to be attentive to this point. Be assured always of my sincere affection for her, and of the special esteem and true consideration with which I have the honor of being, Madame, your very humble, etc.

On this 25 April 1760

I shall write at once to one of my friends, who can put you in touch with Madame de T***. His name is M. G***, First Secretary to Monsieur the Duke of Orléans, who lives in the rue Neuve de Luxembourg, near the rue St. Honoré, in Paris. I shall notify him that you will take the trouble of calling on him, and I shall let him know that I am indebted to you in the extreme, and that I wish for nothing more than to show you my gratitude. He does not ordinarily dine at home.

LETTER
FROM MADAME MADIN
TO M. THE MARQUIS DE CROISMARE

Monsieur, you cannot know how much I have suffered since I last had the honor of writing to you! I have never been able to take it upon myself to confide my sorrow in you, and I hope that you will be grateful to me for having spared your sensitive soul such a painful ordeal. You know how dear she was to me. Imagine, Monsieur, that for close to fifteen days I saw her moving nearer to the end, while in the throes of the most acute pain imaginable. God has at last, I believe, taken pity on her and on me. The poor unfortunate child is still alive, but it won't be for long. Her strength has left her, though in truth the pain has disappeared, but the doctor says it won't do any good. It is a pity; she no longer speaks and has difficulty opening her eyes. The only thing she has left is her patience, which hasn't abandoned her. If she loses that, what will become of us? The hope I had of seeing her cured has suddenly vanished. An abcess had formed on her side and had been surreptitiously growing since her fall; she did not allow us to open it in time, and when she finally agreed, it was too late. She senses the arrival of her last moment, she sends me away and I admit that I am in no condition to withstand that spectacle. She was given the last rites yesterday between ten and half past eleven in the evening; she was the one who asked for them. After this sad ceremony, I kept watch alone next to her bed. She heard me sigh, she looked for my hand, I gave it to her, she took it, placed her lips on it, and drawing me closer to her, said in a voice so low that I had difficulty hearing her: "Mama, just one more favor." "What is it, my child?" "Give me your blessing and leave"... She added: "Monsieur the Marquis... Don't forget to thank him"... These will have been her last words. I gave some orders, and I left to go to a friend's house, where I wait moment by moment. It is one o'clock in the morning. We may by now have a friend in Heaven.

I am respectfully, Monsieur, your very humble, etc.

— Signed, Moreau Madin

The preceding letter was written on May 7th, but it is not dated.

LETTER
FROM MADAME MADIN
TO M. THE MARQUIS DE CROISMARE

The dear child is no longer, her sufferings have ended, and ours will perhaps last for a long time to come. She passed from this world to the one that awaits us all, last Wednesday, between three and four in the morning. Since she had lived an innocent life, her last moments were peaceful, in spite of everything that had been done to disturb them. Allow me to thank you for the tender interest you took in her. This is the last duty that I must fulfill on her behalf. Here are all the letters with which you honored us; I had kept some and found the rest among some papers she gave me a few days before her death. They contain, from what she told me, the story of her life with her parents and in the three convents where she lived, and of everything that happened after she left. There is very little chance of my reading them so soon; I am unable to look at anything that belonged to her, even those things that I gave her out of friendship, without being overwhelmed by sorrow.

If I am ever fortunate enough, Monsieur, to be in a position where I can be of help to you, I will be very flattered if you remember me. I am, Monsieur, with the respect and gratitude that is owed to charitable and benevolent men, your, etc.

—Signed, Moreau Madin

On this 10 May 1760

LETTER
FROM M. THE MARQUIS DE CROISMARE
TO MADAME MADIN

I know, Madame, what it costs a sensitive and benevolent heart when it loses the object of its affection, but also the happiness that can come from doing favors for that object, especially one as worthy, both by virtue of her misfortune and her agreeable qualities, as the dear young lady who is now the cause of your grief. I share that grief with you, Madame, with the most tender sympathy. You knew her, and this is what makes the separation so difficult to endure. Without having had the same advantage, her sufferings touched me deeply, and I was experiencing in advance the pleasure of helping to make her days more peaceful; if Heaven ordered something different for her and has seen fit to deprive me of the satisfaction I so greatly desired, then I must accept it, but I cannot remain indifferent. You at least have the consolation of having acted toward her with the noblest sentiments and the most generous possible conduct; I have admired you for this, and my ambition would have been to imitate you. All that I have left is the fervent desire to have the honor of meeting you and of telling you personally how enchanted I have been by the grandeur of your soul, and with what respectful consideration I have the honor of being, Madame, your very humble, etc.

On this 18 May 1760

Everything that is associated with the memory of our unfortunate child has become extremely precious to me. Would it be asking too great a sacrifice of you to communicate to me the Memoirs and the notes that she took on the subject of her various misfortunes? I ask this favor of you, Madame, with all the more confidence since you had mentioned that I might have some claims to them. I shall faithfully send them back to you, along with the letters, at the earliest opportunity, if you deem it appropriate. Please send them by the Caen coach, which is stabled at the Grand Cerf, rue St. Denis, in Paris, and departs every Monday.

Thus ends the story of the lovable and unfortunate Sister Suzanne Saulier (called Simonin in her account and in this correspondence). It is very sad that the Memoirs of her life were never put into publishable form. They would have made interesting reading. After all, Monsieur the Marquis de Croismare must be grateful to the treachery of his friends for having afforded him the opportunity of rescuing someone in misfortune with a nobility, concern, and simplicity that are truly worthy of him. Indeed the role that he plays in this correspondence is not the least touching one in the novel.

We will perhaps be blamed for having inhumanely hastened the end of Sister Suzanne, but this step had to be taken since word had been sent from the Château de Lasson that a suite of rooms was being furnished for Mademoiselle de Croismare and that her father planned to take her out of the convent where she had been since her mother's death. We had also been informed that a lady's maid was expected to arrive from Paris, who would also be governess to the young lady, and that Monsieur de Croismare was attempting to provide in some other way for the woman who up until that time had been his daughter's maid. This information left us no choice about the measures that had to be taken, and neither the youth, nor the beauty, nor the innocence of Sister Suzanne, nor her gentle, sensitive, and tender nature, capable of touching even the hearts least prone to compassion, were enough to save her from an inevitable death. But since we had all taken on the feelings of Madame Madin for this interesting creature, the grief that her death caused us was hardly less acute than that of her honorable protector.

If there are some slight contradictions between this narrative and the Memoirs, it is because the bulk of the letters were written after the novel; and you will agree that if ever there was a useful preface, it is the one you have just finished reading, and that it is perhaps the only one whose reading should be deferred until the end of the work.

A QUESTION TO MEN OF LETTERS

M. Diderot, after having spent whole mornings composing letters that were well crafted, well thought out, thoroughly romanesque, and laden with pathos, would then spend whole days spoiling those same letters by suppressing, on the advice of his wife and his partners in crime, everything in them that was striking or seemed exaggerated, everything that was not in keeping with the utmost simplicity and verisimilitude; so that if someone had picked up the first group of letters on the street, he would have said: This is beautiful, very beautiful. . . . And if someone had picked up the second group, he would have said: This is very true to life. . . . Which letters were better? Those that might have won admiration? Or those that were certain to produce the illusion?

NOTES

Denis Diderot's complete works (*Oeuvres complètes*, edited by Herbert Dieckmann, Jacques Proust, Jean Varloot et al. [Paris: Hermann, 1975– .]) are cited as DPV.

CHAPTER ONE

1. See James Creech, *Diderot: Thresholds of Representation* (Columbus: Ohio State University Press, 1986); Jack Undank, *Diderot: Inside, Outside, In-between* (Madison, Wisc.: Coda Press, 1979); Jay Caplan, *Framed Narratives: Diderot's Genealogy of the Beholder* (Minneapolis: University of Minnesota Press, 1985); Pierre St. Amand, *Diderot: Le Labyrinthe de la relation* (Paris: Vrin, 1984); Jeffrey Mehlman, *Cataract: A Study in Diderot* (Middletown, Conn.: Wesleyan University Press, 1979); and Thomas M. Kavanagh, *The Vacant Mirror: A Study of Mimesis Through Diderot's "Jacques le fataliste,"* Studies on Voltaire and the Eighteenth Century, vol. 104 (Banbury, Eng.: Voltaire Foundation, 1973).

2. See St. Amand, *Diderot*; and Mehlman, *Cataract*. Another recent study also addresses the problem of order and disorder in Diderot's writings, but does so from a more traditional perspective; see Geoffrey Bremner, *Order and Chance: The Pattern of Diderot's Thought* (New York: Cambridge University Press, 1983).

3. See, e.g., Ilya Prigogine and Isabelle Stengers, *La Nouvelle Alliance: Métamorphoses de la science* (Paris: Gallimard, 1979), trans. as *Order out of Chaos: Man's New Dialogue with Nature* (New York: Bantam Books, 1984); and Henri Atlan, *Entre le Cristal et la fumée: Essai sur l'organisation du vivant*

(Paris: Seuil, 1979). For an incisive critical overview of the "new paradigm" theorized in the work of Atlan and others, see Jean-Pierre Dupuy, *Ordres et désordres: Enquête sur un nouveau paradigme* (Paris: Seuil, 1982).

4. This is most notably the case in the work of Michel Serres. See his *La Naissance de la physique dans le texte de Lucrèce* (Paris: Minuit, 1977); *La Communication* (Paris: Minuit, 1968); and *Le Parasite* (Paris: Grasset, 1980), trans. Lawrence R. Schehr as *The Parasite* (Baltimore: Johns Hopkins University Press, 1982).

5. See Prigogine and Stengers, *Order out of Chaos*.

6. See *Entre le Cristal et la fumée*.

7. Dupuy, *Ordres et désordres*, 117.

8. See, e.g., J. R. Pierce, *Symbols, Signals and Noise: The Nature and Process of Communication* (New York: Harper and Brothers, 1961).

9. Serres, "Le Dialogue platonicien et la genèse intersubjective de l'abstraction" in *La Communication*, 40, trans. as "Platonic Dialogue," in *Hermes: Literature, Science, Philosophy*, ed. Josué V. Harari and David F. Bell (Baltimore: Johns Hopkins University Press, 1982), 66.

10. Ibid., 66–67.

11. Herbert Dieckmann, "The *Préface-annexe* of *La Religieuse*," *Diderot Studies* 2 (1952): 21–40.

CHAPTER TWO

1. Recent studies devoted exclusively to the *Préface-annexe* are Jacques Chouillet, "La Vertu malheureuse," in his *Diderot* (Paris: SEDES, 1977), 177–88, a study of the role the letters of the *Préface-annexe* play in granting "authenticity" to Diderot's account of Suzanne Simonin's life in the *Préface-annexe*; Georges May, "Quelques nouveaux éclaircissements sur la mystification du Marquis de Croismare," in *Essays on Diderot and the Enlightenment in Honor of Otis Fellows*, ed. John Pappas (Geneva: Droz, 1974), 182–96, a study of the proper names in the *Préface-annexe*; and Jean Varloot, "*La Religieuse* et sa *Préface*," in *Studies in the French Eighteenth Century Presented to John Lough*, ed. D. J. Mossop et al. (Durham, Eng.: University of Durham Press, 1978), 260–70. Varloot explores the question of whether the *Préface-annexe* should follow or precede *La Religieuse*, arguing in favor of the latter and concluding that *La Religieuse* along with its preface should be considered "a double work"

(p. 268). In addition, three recent studies provide detailed accounts of the past and present controversies surrounding the *Préface-annexe*: Herbert Dieckmann's and Georges May's introductions to the new critical edition of *La Religieuse* (vol. 11 of DPV, 3–23) as well as the chapter entitled "Origins" in Vivienne Mylne, *Diderot: La Religieuse* (London: Grant & Cutler, 1981), 9–13.

2. Although the text attributes this narration to Grimm, we shall see that it is also possible to attribute it to Diderot.

3. Denis Diderot, "'Préface' de *La Religieuse*," in DPV, 11: 33. Subsequent references in the text are to this edition. A complete translation of the *Préface* can be found in the Appendix to the present work.

4. For in-depth analyses of the characteristics of the epistolary genre, see Tzvetan Todorov, *Littérature et signification* (Paris: Larousse, 1967); Laurent Versini, *Le Roman épistolaire* (Paris: Presses Universitaires de France, 1979); Janet G. Altman, *Epistolarity: Approaches to a Form* (Columbus: Ohio State University Press, 1982); and Ronald C. Rosbottom, "Motifs in Epistolary Fiction: Analysis of a Narrative Subgenre," *L'Esprit créateur* 17, no. 4 (1977): 279–301.

5. This letter is emblematic of every one of Suzanne's attempts to communicate in the actual body of *La Religieuse*, as we shall see in Chapter 3.

6. Here Diderot applies to a literary text a strategy he had once advised Greuze to use in his paintings. In Jack Undank's summary of a passage from the *Salon* of 1767: "Put a figure of the artist, [Diderot] says, *in* the painting; make him look as though he were filled with tenderness and moved at the sight of his model. The viewer will borrow his reaction from this artist, a surrogate of the artist outside the work" (*Diderot: Inside, Outside, In-between* [Madison, Wisc.: Coda Press, 1979], 36, 23n).

7. The Marquis's reluctant response: "I am mortified that I am unable to contribute to the execution of the project you are contemplating on her behalf; without knowing more about it, I can only judge its worth by the prudence of which you are capable and by the interest that you take in it. I have circulated very little in Paris, and only among a small number of persons who circulate as little as I, and acquaintances of the kind you desire are not easy to find" (52).

8. Georges May also identifies Suzanne's reference to the guardian angel as the source of the disagreement between Diderot and Grimm, although he frames the problem in different terms, claiming that Su-

zanne's misinterpretation of the seal not only lacks verisimilitude but also implies too much ingenuousness on her part: "Even though Grimm doesn't indicate what it was in the preceding letter that risked giving everything away, we can speculate that it was the excess of naiveté that inspired the nun's unexpected and comic notion of taking Cupid for a guardian angel" (41, 25*n*).

9. The problem of Diderot and his reader is explored in three important critical studies: Herbert Dieckmann, "Diderot et son lecteur," in idem, *Cinq leçons sur Diderot* (Geneva: Droz, 1959), 15–40; Undank, *Inside, Outside, and In-between*; and James Creech, "Diderot and the Pleasure of the Other: Friends, Readers and Posterity," *Eighteenth-Century Studies* 11, no. 4 (1978): 439–56. Unlike these critics, however, I am not concerned with the capital role the imagined reader plays in Diderot's ability to create, nor with the larger philosophical problem of self and other and its role in the constitution (or subversion) of Diderot's literary subjectivity. Rather, I am interested in identifying and describing the specific mechanisms Diderot builds into his texts in an attempt to draw the actual reader in. (My own thinking about the problem of the relationship between reader and text in Diderot was sparked initially by discussions with Herbert Dieckmann, whose memory lingers in these pages.)

10. This is an instance of the *Préface-annexe*'s deviation from the conventions of the epistolary genre, which in its classical form generally grants the reader a privileged perspective, positioning him or her in such a way that, as Jean Rousset observes, "only the reader is in a position to reconstitute [the whole]" (*Narcisse romancier: Essai sur la première personne dans le roman* [Paris: José Corti, 1973], 21).

11. This incorporation of the reader into the universe of the fiction has some striking analogies in Diderot's writings on art, notably in the *Salons* devoted to Vernet's landscapes. To describe a particular painting, Diderot adopts the vantage point not of an observer who stands before it but rather of someone who, in a sense, has entered the painting and is circulating within it. For an analysis of this trait of Diderot's *Salons* and its relationship to the larger issues posed by Diderot's theories of beholding, see Michael Fried's definitive study, *Absorption and Theatricality: Painting and Beholder in the Age of Diderot* (Berkeley: University of California Press, 1980).

12. Georges May, *Diderot et "La Religieuse"* (New Haven: Yale University Press, 1954), 36, 37. May revised his position on the issue of the historical actuality of the events recounted in the *Préface-annexe* after Dieckmann published his analysis of the autograph manuscript of the *Préface-annexe* in the Fonds Vandeul. I am using May's earlier essay only as an exemplar of a critic in the process of reading Diderot's text. For May's current position, see his Introduction to vol. 11 of DPV, 3–12.

13. May, *Diderot et "La Religieuse,"* 40–41 (my translation).

14. Herbert Dieckmann, "The *Préface-annexe* of *La Religieuse*," *Diderot Studies* 2 (1952): 31. Although Dieckmann and other critics of *La Religieuse* generally assume that Grimm was the author of the first version of the *Préface-annexe* (the version that Diderot subsequently revised in 1780–81 and to which he added new passages), my hunch is that *Diderot* was its author and not Grimm, although to my knowledge there is no archival evidence that either supports or disproves this hunch (at least not according to the secondary sources I have read and my own examination of two manuscripts of the *Préface-annexe*: the version that appeared in the *Correspondance littéraire* in 1770 [Bibliothèque historique de la ville de Paris] and a later version in a volume allegedly containing passages suppressed from the *Correspondance littéraire* [Bibliothèque de l'Arsenal]). Nevertheless, I think the textual mechanisms I have outlined imply that it was Diderot who composed this text and that Grimm is just another fictional character in a *mise-en-abyme* of hypostatized readers.

15. Ibid., 28.

16. Ibid.

17. Chouillet, "La Vertu malheureuse," 187–88. Chouillet's essay is particularly pertinent to the subject of the present study, for in it he again reminds us, as Dieckmann had done earlier in the article in question, that the *Préface-annexe* should not be read literally.

18. Dieckmann, "The *Préface-annexe* of *La Religieuse*," 28–29.

19. Ibid., 34.

20. Michel Foucault, "Qu'est-ce qu'un auteur?" *Bulletin de la Société Française de Philosophie* 63, no. 3 (1969), translated and expanded as "What Is an Author?" in *Textual Strategies: Perspectives in Post-Structuralist Criticism*, ed. Josué V. Harari (Ithaca: Cornell University Press, 1980), 159.

21. Denis Diderot, "Eloge de Richardson," in DPV, 13: 192–208.

22. Ibid., 193.
23. Ibid., 198.
24. Dieckmann, "The *Préface-annexe* of *La Religieuse*," 34.

CHAPTER THREE

1. Denis Diderot, *The Nun* (New York: Viking Penguin, 1974), 109; and idem, *La Religieuse* in DPV, 11: 192. Subsequent references in the text are to these editions. The first number refers to the English translation; the second to the French original. I have altered the English translation in some places to bring it closer to the original and to allow me to highlight certain crucial features of the text.

The critical literature on *La Religieuse* is too vast to cite exhaustively, but I would like to signal several important recent studies devoted wholly or in part to this novel: the two chapters on *La Religieuse* in Jay Caplan, *Framed Narratives: Diderot's Genealogy of the Beholder* (Minneapolis: University of Minnesota Press, 1985), 45–75; Walter E. Rex, "Secrets from Suzanne: The Tangled Motives of *La Religieuse*," in idem, *The Attraction of the Contrary: Essays on the Literature of the French Enlightenment* (New York: Cambridge University Press, 1987), 125–35; Flavio Luoni, "*La Religieuse*: Récit et écriture du corps," *Littérature* 54 (1984): 79–99; Herbert Josephs, "Diderot's *La Religieuse*: Libertinism and the Dark Cave of the Soul," *MLN* 91 (1976): 734–55; David Marshall, "*La Religieuse*: Sympathy and Seduction," in idem, *The Surprising Effects of Sympathy* (Chicago: Chicago University Press, 1988), 84–104; and three articles from *Diderot: Digression and Dispersion*, ed. Jack Undank and Herbert Josephs (Lexington, Ky.: French Forum, 1984): Jack Undank, "An Ethics of Discourse," 231–49; Carol Sherman, "Changing Spaces," 219–30; and Beatrice Fink, "Des Mets et des mots de Suzanne," 98–105.

2. Michael Fried has noted the frequent appearance of absorptive *tableaux* in *La Religieuse*: "A pursuit of absorptive effects characterizes French literary pictorialism in the 1760's. Such effects are especially vivid in Diderot's novel *La Religieuse* (composed 1760), about which he wrote to Meister in 1780: 'It is filled with pathos-laden *tableaux*. It is very interesting, and all the interest is focused on the character who is speaking. . . . It is a work to be perused ceaselessly by painters; and if it were not forbidden by modesty, its true epigraph would be *son pittor anch'io*' " (*Absorption and Theatricality: Painting and Beholder in the Age of Diderot* [Berke-

ley: University of California Press, 1980], 199–200). My readings of both the *Préface-annexe* and *La Religieuse* owe a large intellectual debt to Fried's work on Diderot, and most notably to his *Absorption and Theatricality*. For an analysis of the rhetorical function of literary *tableaux* in Diderot's writings, see Caplan, *Framed Narratives*.

3. Wilhelm Leibniz, *The Monadology* in *The Monadology and Other Philosophical Writings*, trans. Robert Latta (Oxford: Oxford University Press, 1968), 246.

4. Michel Serres, *The Parasite*, trans. Lawrence R. Schehr (Baltimore: Johns Hopkins University Press, 1982), 43.

5. For insightful discussions of Diderot's views on music, see the chapter entitled "The Figure of Music in the Frontispiece of Diderot's *Encyclopédie*," in Rex, *Attraction of the Contrary*, 108–24; Béatrice Didier, "Le Texte de la musique," in *Interpréter Diderot aujourd'hui*, ed. Elisabeth de Fontenay and Jacques Proust (Paris: Le Sycomore, 1984), 287–317; and John Neubauer, "Absolute and Affective Music: Rameau, Diderot, and Goethe," in *Johann Wolfgang von Goethe: One Hundred and Fifty Years of Continuing Vitality*, ed. Ulrich Goebel and Wolodymyr T. Zyla (Lubbock: Texas Tech Press, 1984), 115–31.

6. Michel Serres, "Platonic Dialogue," in *Hermes: Literature, Science, Philosophy*, ed. Josué V. Harari and David F. Bell (Baltimore: Johns Hopkins University Press, 1982), 66–67.

7. Roland Barthes, *S/Z*, trans. Richard Miller (New York: Farrar, Straus and Giroux, 1974), 145.

8. On the characteristics of first-person retrospective narration, see the chapter entitled "Voix" in Gérard Genette, *Figures III* (Paris: Seuil, 1972), 225–67. See also Philippe Lejeune, *Le Pacte autobiographique* (Paris: Seuil, 1975); and Jean Rousset, *Narcisse romancier: Essai sur la première personne dans le roman* (Paris: José Corti, 1973).

9. See, e.g., Jean Parrish, "Conception, évolution, et forme finale de *La Religieuse*," *Romanische Forschungen* 74 (1962): 361–84; Emile Lizé, "*La Religieuse*, un roman épistolaire?" *Studies on Voltaire and the Eighteenth Century* 98 (1972): 143–63; Georges May, *Diderot et "La Religieuse"* (New Haven: Yale University Press, 1954), 205–15; and Vivienne Mylne, "Diderot," in idem, *The Eighteenth-Century French Novel: Techniques and Illusion* (New York: Barnes and Noble, 1965), 192–220.

10. See Georges May's complete inventory of the famous "blunders" in Suzanne's narrative in *Diderot et "La Religieuse."* See also Roger

Lewinter, *Oeuvres complètes de Diderot* (Paris: Club Français du Livre, 1969–73), 4: 504–6; Jean Catrysse, *Diderot et la mystification* (Paris: Nizet, 1970), 224–29; and Mylne, "Diderot," as well as Mylne's more recent "What Suzanne Knew: Lesbianism and *La Religieuse*," *Studies on Voltaire and the Eighteenth Century* 208 (1982): 167–73.

11. May, *Diderot et "La Religieuse*," 206.

12. The episodes in question are (1) the passage that appears at the end of the description of Suzanne's first encounter with the lesbian mother superior: "[The superior] said a hundred sweet nothings to me and lavished on me a thousand caresses that embarrassed me a little, why I don't know, for I did not understand what was happening and neither did she. And even now, when I think back to it, what could we have understood?" (126; 214); and (2) "I don't know what can be imagined about one woman and another" (86; 164). See May's editorial footnotes 92 and 68 to the text of *La Religieuse* in DPV, 11: 214, 293.

13. Herbert Dieckmann, Introduction to the *Préface* of *La Religieuse*, in DPV, 11: 21.

14. In "What Suzanne Knew," Vivienne Mylne, interestingly, revises her earlier position on the question of Diderot's "blunders" and argues instead that Suzanne's sexual innocence has a logic of its own. Though it is a logic different from the one I have been describing, Mylne agrees that Suzanne's innocence does not need to be viewed as an inconsistency in the narrative of *La Religieuse*.

15. Paul Robert, *Le Petit Robert: Dictionnaire alphabétique et analogique de la langue française* (Paris: Société du Nouveau Littré, 1969), 589.

16. For a thorough discussion of this issue and a detailed inventory of the chronological incongruities in *La Religieuse*, see Philip Stewart, "A Note on Chronology in *La Religieuse*," *Romance Notes* 12 (1970–71): 149–56.

17. Interestingly, Michel Foucault reads this feature of the text not as a flaw, but as an instance of self-reflexivity in language, of the text pointing to its own ontological status as language. For him Madame Simonin's letter is "a sign that language is speaking of itself, that the letter is not the letter, but the language which doubles it within the same system of reality.... Diderot's 'blunder' is not the result of his eagerness to intervene, but is due to the opening of language to its system of self-representation: the letter in *The Nun* is only an analogue of a letter, resembling it in every detail with the exception of being its imperceptibly

displaced double (this displacement made visible only because of a tear in the fabric of language)" ("Language to Infinity," in idem, *Language, Counter-Memory, Practice: Selected Essays and Interviews* [Ithaca: Cornell University Press, 1977], 57–58).

18. May, *Diderot et "La Religieuse,"* 207–8.

19. Stewart, "A Note on Chronology," 154–55.

20. Of the many excellent books and articles written on *Jacques le fataliste*, I have found five particularly helpful: Thomas M. Kavanagh, *The Vacant Mirror: A Study of Mimesis Through Diderot's "Jacques le fataliste," Studies on Voltaire and the Eighteenth Century*, vol. 104 (Banbury, Eng.: Voltaire Foundation, 1973); idem, "*Jacques le fataliste*: An Encyclopedia of the Novel," in *Diderot: Digression and Dispersion*, 150–65; Marie-Hélène Huet, "*Jacques le fataliste*," in idem, *Le Héros et son double: Essai sur le roman d'ascension sociale au XVIIIe siècle* (Paris: José Corti, 1975), 105–26; Jack Undank, *Diderot: Inside, Outside and In-between* (Madison, Wisc.: Coda Press, 1979); and Aram Vartanian, "*Jacques le fataliste*: A Journey into the Ramifications of a Dilemma," in *Essays on Diderot and the Enlightenment in Honor of Otis Fellows*, ed. John Pappas (Geneva: Droz, 1974), 325–47.

21. Denis Diderot, *Jacques the Fatalist and His Master*, trans. Michael Henry (New York: Viking Penguin, 1986), 51; and Denis Diderot, *Jacques le fataliste*, in DPV, 23: 58. Subsequent references in the text are to these editions. The first number refers to the English translation; the second to the French original. I have altered the English translation in some places to bring it closer to the original and to allow me to highlight certain crucial features of the text.

22. Pierre St. Amand takes a different though complementary approach to the problem of noise in *Jacques le fataliste*. See his "Jacques le fataliste ou Jacques le parasite," *Stanford French Review* 11, no. 1 (1987): 99–111.

23. May, *Diderot et "La Religieuse,"* 218.

24. Ibid.

25. Serres, *The Parasite*, 12.

26. Herbert Dieckmann, Introduction to the *Préface* of *La Religieuse*, in DPV, 11: 21.

CHAPTER FOUR

1. On the relationship between narrative patterns and the writing of history, see Lionel Gossman, *Between History and Literature* (Cambridge: Harvard University Press, 1990); and idem, "History and Literature: Reproduction or Signification," in *The Writing of History: Literary Form and Historical Understanding*, ed. Robert H. Canary and Henry Kozicki (Madison: University of Wisconsin Press, 1978), 3–39; Hayden White, "The Historical Text as Literary Artifact," in *The Writing of History*, 41–62; and Paul Veyne, *Comment on écrit l'histoire* (Paris: Seuil, 1978).

2. J. Robert Loy, "*L'Essai sur les règnes de Claude et de Néron*," *Cahiers de l'Association internationale des études françaises* 13 (June 1961): 254, 239. For an excellent résumé of the traditional criticism of the *Essai*, as well as cogent arguments against the conclusions of critics who claim that the *Essai* is an inferior work, see Jean-Marie Goulemot, "Jeux de conscience, de texte et de philosophie: L'Art de prendre des positions dans l'*Essai sur les règnes de Claude et de Néron* de Denis Diderot," *Revue des sciences humaines* 182 (1981): 45–53. See also Jean Starobinski's insightful "Diderot et la parole des autres," *Critique* 296 (1972): 3–22; Herbert Josephs, "*Essai sur les règnes de Claude et de Néron*: A Final Borrowing," in *Diderot: Digression and Dispersion*, ed. Jack Undank and Herbert Josephs (Lexington, Ky.: French Forum, 1984), 138–49; William T. Conroy, Jr., *Diderot's "Essai sur Sénèque,"* *Studies on Voltaire and the Eighteenth Century*, vol. 131 (Banbury, Eng.: Voltaire Foundation, 1975); John Hope Mason, "Portrait de l'auteur, accompagné d'un fantôme: *L'Essai sur les règnes de Claude et de Néron*," in *Diderot: Les Dernières Années*, ed. Peter France and Anthony Strugnell (Edinburgh: Edinburgh University Press, 1985), 43–62; Douglas A. Bonneville, *Diderot's Vie de Sénèque: A Swan Song Revised* (Gainesville: University of Florida Press, 1966); and Roger Lewinter, Introduction to Denis Diderot, *Essai sur les règnes de Claude et de Néron, et sur les moeurs et les écrits de Sénèque* (Paris: Union Générale d'Edition, 1972), 9–31.

3. On Diderot's contributions to Raynal's *Histoire*, see Michèle Duchet's authoritative *Diderot et l'Histoire des Deux Indes ou l'écriture fragmentaire* (Paris: Nizet, 1978). For the details of the collaboration between Raynal and Diderot, I am indebted to Duchet's book. See also Anthony Strugnell, "La Voix du sage dans l'*Histoire des Deux Indes*," in *Diderot: Les Dernières Années*, 30–42.

4. Duchet, *Diderot et l'Histoire des Deux Indes*, 161.
5. Guillaume Thomas Francis Raynal, *Histoire philosophique et politique des établissements et du commerce des Européens dans les Deux Indes* (Geneva: Jean-Léonard Pellet, 1783), vol. 1, Books 1–27. I shall henceforth cite this work as *Histoire des Deux Indes*.
6. Ibid., 191–92.
7. Duchet, *Diderot et l'Histoire des Deux Indes*, 10.
8. Ibid., 194.
9. Denis Diderot, *Le Rêve de d'Alembert*, in DPV, 17: 110.
10. *Histoire des Deux Indes*, 8: 5. I attribute to Diderot only those passages that Michèle Duchet has identified as being his. For a complete listing of Diderot's contributions to the *Histoire des Deux Indes*, see the chapter entitled "Dispersion et regroupements: Les tableaux," in Duchet's *Diderot et l'Histoire des Deux Indes*, 49–155.
11. *Histoire des Deux Indes*, 5: 6.
12. This observation echoes the passage in the *Rêve de d'Alembert* in which Diderot insists that it is impossible to extrapolate from present events those that took place in the past or that will take place in the future. Using as an example the evolution of animals, he writes: "If man isn't separated out into an infinity of men, he separates out, at least, into an infinity of animalcules whose future and final metamorphoses and organization are impossible to foresee. Who knows if this might not be the seedbed of a second generation of beings, removed from this one by an unfathomable interval of centuries and successive developments?" (Diderot, *Le Rêve de d'Alembert*, 126).
13. *Histoire des Deux Indes*, 5: 5–6.
14. Ibid., 230.
15. Ibid., 231.
16. Ibid.
17. Denis Diderot, *Essai sur les règnes de Claude et de Néron*, in DPV, 25: 292. Subsequent references in the text are to this edition.
18. "Louis XV had made the three statements recalled [here]: the first, at the time of the transfer, which he desired, of the Hôtel-Dieu to the Ile des Cygnes; the second, about his minister, M. de Monteynard; the third, on several different occasions." Assézat also quotes Grimm on Diderot's daring to include this passage in the *Essai*: "Freedom [of speech] was taken very far in several parts of this reedition, as in the parallel between Claudius's character and that of a king who is not difficult

to recognize, since remarks that everyone knows to be his are quoted." See the *Essai sur les règnes de Claude et de Néron*, in *Oeuvres complètes*, ed. J. Assézat (Paris: Garnier, 1875), 3: 37.

19. Starobinski, "Diderot et la parole des autres," 7–8.

20. Starobinski, for example, argues: "Pleading in favor of Seneca will amount, for Diderot, to killing two birds with one stone: he will defend philosophy from the antiphilosophers, and he will defend himself from the accusations of a guilty conscience" (ibid., 7), though Jean Ehrard disagrees with this interpretation and claims: "Supposing that [Diderot] . . . really had had illusions about the Empress's willingness to make reforms . . . all illusions had certainly vanished by the time he began to draft the *Essai* . . . But nothing . . . authorizes [us] to change a disappointment into feelings of guilt" (Preface to the *Essai sur les règnes de Claude et de Néron*, in DPV, 25: 11). In general, however, critics tend to agree with Starobinski's contention; see, e.g., Goulemot, "Jeux de conscience," 49; and Conroy, *Diderot's "Essai sur Sénèque,"* 92.

21. Starobinski notes: "The presence of others is fundamentally a spoken presence. Hence the polyphonic aspect of the *Essai*" ("Diderot et la parole des autres," 8).

22. As Jean-Marie Goulemot notes, "This *we* facilitates the merging of the philosopher and the reader, and also allows the reader to hoist himself up next to the philosopher, himself settled within the intimate shadow of Seneca" ("Jeux de conscience," 52).

23. *Encyclopédie ou dictionnaire raisonné des sciences, des arts et des métiers* (New York: Pergamon Press, n.d.), 2: 335–37.

24. On Voltaire's notion of history, see Gossman, "History and Literature"; and Maureen F. O'Meara, "Towards a Typology of Historical Discourse: The Case of Voltaire," *MLN* 93 (1978): 938–62.

25. For a different though complementary analysis of conversational models in Diderot, see Christie V. McDonald, *The Dialogue of Writing: Essays in Eighteenth-Century French Literature* (Waterloo, Ontario: Wilfrid Laurier University Press, 1984).

CHAPTER FIVE

1. Among the many texts I found particularly helpful when studying the *Rêve de d'Alembert* were Wilda Anderson, "Diderot's Laboratory of Sensibility," *Yale French Studies* 67 (1984): 72–91; Herbert Dieckmann,

"The Metaphoric Structure of the *Rêve de d'Alembert*," *Diderot Studies* 17 (1973): 15–24; Georges Daniel, "Autour du *Rêve de d'Alembert*: Réflexions sur l'esthétique de Diderot," *Diderot Studies* 12 (1969): 13–73; Yvon Belaval, "Trois lectures du *Rêve de d'Alembert*," *Diderot Studies* 18 (1975): 15–32; Aram Vartanian, "Diderot and the Phenomenology of the Dream," *Diderot Studies* 8 (1966): 217–53; and the chapters "L'Essaim d'abeilles" and "Le Clavecin-philosophe," in Jacques Chouillet, *Diderot: Poète de l'énergie* (Paris: Presses Universitaires de France, 1984), 226–78.

2. Denis Diderot, *Le Rêve de d'Alembert*, in DPV, 17: 119. Subsequent references in the text are to this edition. Throughout this chapter I shall substitute the term *sensibility* for *sensibilité* and the term *sensate* for *sensible*; I shall provide Diderot's own definition of both terms further on.

3. This notion also appears in Diderot's *Principes philosophiques sur la matière et le mouvement*, where he states: "The supposition that there is any kind of being at all situated outside the material universe is an impossibility. One must never make such suppositions, because one can never infer anything from them" (DPV, 17: 19).

4. For an incisive and comprehensive analysis of Diderot's materialism, see Wilda Anderson, *Diderot's Dream* (Baltimore: Johns Hopkins University Press, 1990).

5. Denis Diderot, *Eléments de physiologie*, in DPV, 17: 305.

6. Paul Robert, *Le Petit Robert: Dictionnaire alphabétique et analogique de la langue française* (Paris: Société du Nouveau Littré, 1969), 878.

7. Jean Varloot, in his edition of the *Rêve de d'Alembert*, also notes that "in classical physics *impression* carries the meaning of pressure" (DPV, 17: 155, 200*n*).

8. In the *Dictionnaire de Trévoux* of the time, *s'arranger* (here translated as "straightening itself out") means "mettre en bon ordre" (to put in good order).

9. Or, as the character Diderot puts it at a different point: "sensibility, a general property of matter or a product of organization" (105). For an in-depth analysis of the role of sensibility in the organization of living matter, see Anderson, "Diderot's Laboratory of Sensibility"; and especially chap. 2 of her more recent *Diderot's Dream*.

10. For another perspective on the relationship between nutrition and generation in the *Rêve de d'Alembert*, see Jean Starobinski, "Le Philosophe, le géomètre, l'hybride," *Poétique* 21 (1975): 8–23. On the prob-

lem of the relationship between eating and sensibility, see Beatrice Fink, "Des Mets et des mots de Suzanne," in *Diderot: Digression and Dispersion*, ed. Jack Undank and Herbert Josephs (Lexington, Ky.: French Forum, 1984), 98–105.

11. One could even extend this to say that sensibility in this case takes on a function similar to that of the Leibnizian God.

12. Diderot even alludes subtly to d'Alembert's "pulverization" at the end of the conversation in an ironic variation on a theological theme: "Good night, my friend, *et memento quia pulvis es, et in pulverem reverteris* [and remember that thou art dust and to dust thou shalt return]" (113).

13. The term Diderot uses, *molécules*, does not carry the modern meaning; here *molécules* means very small—almost primitive—units.

14. This exchange does not actually appear in the text. We learn about it indirectly through Mademoiselle, who retells its principal events to Bordeu at the beginning of the second dialogue.

15. This is another sign of the change in her condition, for as Mademoiselle has already noted by observing d'Alembert, agitation is one of the "symptoms" of active sensibility. Mademoiselle tells Bordeu, for example, that d'Alembert "spent a most agitated night" (115) and subsequently describes d'Alembert's agitation to Bordeu in these terms: "When he went to bed, instead of resting as he ordinarily does, for he sleeps like a child, he began to toss and turn, to stretch out his arms, to throw off the covers, and to speak aloud" (116). And, at a later point, d'Alembert himself describes the night he has just spent in the same terms: "I don't believe I've ever spent a more agitated night than this one" (144).

16. "Look at your sheet of paper and listen to me" (121). Bordeu's formulation of d'Alembert's utterings is so exact that at the end of his speech Mademoiselle rings for d'Alembert's servants and interrogates them, suspecting that one of them had shown Bordeu her transcript before his arrival: "I can't get over it. You see, Doctor, I suspected [one of the servants] of having given you my scribblings" (124).

17. Noise in both Serres and Diderot is a material entity. But when Serres says that "background noise" is the third term that both interrupts and facilitates communication, what becomes important is not the effect that that noise has on the *body* of the interlocutors—other than that the noise makes it hard for them to hear each other—but the

bond that is established between the interlocutors as a result of their joint effort to block out the auditory interference. In Diderot, the sounds quite literally enter the bodies of the interlocutors and trigger a series of physiological reactions, reactions that ultimately effect a change in the interlocutors' intellectual perspective.

18. For the opposing view that reads Diderot as a dualist, the standard reference is still Aram Vartanian, *Descartes and Diderot: A Study of Scientific Naturalism in the Enlightenment* (Princeton: Princeton University Press, 1953). For a clever modern update, see Vartanian's article "Diderot, or the Dualist in Spite of Himself" in *Diderot: Digression and Dispersion*, 250–68.

19. Mademoiselle's reaction is reminiscent of Diderot's description of Suzanne Simonin's response to the sexual advances of the mother superior in *La Religieuse*: "I don't know what was going on inside me; I was afraid, my heart was pounding, I had difficulty breathing, I was upset, oppressed, agitated; I was frightened, my strength seemed to have left me, and I was about to faint. And yet I cannot say it was pain I was feeling" (*La Religieuse*, 138; 228).

20. Denis Diderot, *Lettres à Sophie Volland*, ed. André Babelon (Paris: Gallimard, 1930), 3: 209.

21. Jean Starobinski, "Diderot et la parole des autres," *Critique* 296 (1972): 14–15.

INDEX

In this index an "f" after a number indicates a separate reference on the next page, and an "ff" indicates separate references on the next two pages. A continuous discussion over two or more pages is indicated by a span of page numbers, e.g., "57–59." *Passim* is used for a cluster of references in close but not consecutive sequence.

Absorptive effects, 68–69, 171–72, 218n2
Action, in Richardson's novels, 35
Ambiguity, 55, 92
Analogy, historical, 94–98
Aristarques, 120
Assézat, Jules, 94, 223n18
Atlan, Henri, 5
Authority: authorial, 20–21, 32; in *Préface-annexe*, 20–25

Barthes, Roland, 55
Bee swarm, 130–31, 132–33
Biography, political history as, 92
Body, effect of sounds on, 142–43, 149–50, 227n17
Bordeu (character), 138f, 150–61

Catherine II of Russia, 96
Causality: historical narrative structure and, 86, 92; nature and, 88–90; time and, 89, 107–8, 138–39
Chouillet, Jacques, 30, 217n17
Chronological order, 85–86, 87, 93, 107–8. *See also* Present-past relation
Communication model: Leibnizian, 50–51, 62; spatial vs. temporal, 62–63. *See also* Ternary model of communication
Communication theory, disorder in, 5–7. *See also* Serres, Michel
Conspirators in *Préface-annexe*: ternary structure and, 13; progressive internalization and,

17–27, 171; objectivity of, 21–23, 24–25; reader and, 25–27
Contact, and sensibility, 135–36, 141–48 *passim*, 153–54
Contagiousness: as quality of sensibility, 160–61; of affective states, 171–73
Croismare, Marquis de (character), 22

D'Alainville anecdote, 19, 28–29, 30–31, 32
D'Alembert (character), activation of sensibility in, 140–45, 226n12, 226n16
De l'Espinasse, Mademoiselle (character): activation of sensibility in, 146–49; Bordeu's conversations with, 150–61
De Moni, Madame (character), 44–47, 50–51, 62, 171
Destabilization: of reader-author relation, 33–38; of retrospective narration, 55–63; of ternary model, 61–63; of position of reader, 107–8, 116
Detail, Richardson's use of, 35–36
Dialogue: noise in, 6–7; Serres's definition of, 52–53; material processes and, 140–49 *passim*; interpenetration of sensibility and, 154–56. *See also* Direct communication
Diderot, Denis: as author vs. character in *Préface-annexe*, 14–15, 18–21, 32; historical narrative approach of, 86–92; contemporary opponents of, 119–21; writings on art, 215n6, 216n11; historical writings, *see Essai sur les règnes de Claude et de Néron*; *Histoire des Deux Indes* (Raynal) — works; *Eléments de physiologie*, 129, 172; "Eloge de Richardson," 34, 35–37; *Encyclopédie*, 32, 115–16; *Essai sur les règnes de Claude et de Néron*, 93–123; *Pensées sur l'interprétation de la nature*, 89; *Préface-annexe* of *La Religieuse*, 11–38; *Principes philosophiques sur la matière et le mouvement*, 225n3; *Religieuse, La*, 41–79; *Rêve de d'Alembert, Le*, 127–66; *Salons*, 216n11. *See also specific works by title*
Dieckmann, Herbert, 7–8, 28, 29–32, 36, 58, 216n9
Direct communication, futility of, 42–44, 48, 160
Disorder: scientific theory and, 3–5; communication theory and, 5–7
Double entendre, 55
Dreaming, 145
Duchet, Michèle, 223n10
Duration, and sensibility, 131–32, 153–54

Eating, 136–38, 145, 225n10
Ehrard, Jean, 224n20
Enlightenment philosophy, 115, 119–20
Epistolary genre: binary vs. ter-

nary exchange in, 11–13; ineffectiveness of binary exchange in, 42; position of reader in, 216n10. *See also* Narrative structure

Errors, *see* Inconsistencies

Essai sur les règnes de Claude et de Néron (Diderot), 83, 93–123; narrative structure in, 93; present-past relation in, 94–98, 99–100; reader in, 104–7, 169, 174; ternary model and, 104–16; Diderot's opponents and, 119–21; Diderot's goal in writing of, 123; contagious affective links and, 172–73; critical literature on, 222n2

Exclusion, *see* Inclusion-exclusion dynamic

Falconet anecdote, 134–35
Fiction, theory of, 37–38
Foucault, Michel, 32, 220n17
Fried, Michael, 68, 218n2

Gender, in Diderot's writings, 25n
Generative processes: new ideas and, 119, 164–66; transformation from inert to active sensibility and, 133–36, 137–38; eating as prototype for, 136–38; time in, 138–39
God: mediation of communication by, 50–51, 62; nature and, 128–29, 137, 139; sensibility as substitute for, 139–40, 226n11

Goulemot, Jean-Marie, 224n22
Grimm, M. (character): as narrative authority, 11–14 *passim*, 20–25; role in plot, 14, 17f; as witness, 19, 25–27; as assumed author of *Préface-annexe*, 217n14

Harpsichord-philosopher analogy, 129–30, 131
Histoire des Deux Indes (Raynal), 83, 84–93; Diderot's contributions to, 85, 86–87, 223n10; distinct voices of, 100f, 103; temporality in, 114
Historical knowledge: causal models and, 89–90; unreadability and, 90–91; biographical approach and, 91–92; reconstruction of past events and, 104, 107–8, 109
Historical periods, similarities between, 94–98, 99–100
Historical writing, conventional: temporality in, 85–86; relation of reader, historian, and past and, 109–11, 115
Historical writings of Diderot, *see Essai sur les règnes de Claude et de Néron*; *Histoire des Deux Indes* (Raynal)
Human nervous system, 148–49

Impression, as term, 130f, 225n7
Inclusion-exclusion dynamic, 163
Inconsistencies: logical, 56–60, 172, 219n10; temporal, 63–65,

66–67; narrative function of, 77–78, 220n17

Indirection: prayer as communication and, 44–48, 50–51, 62, 68; music and, 48–50, 51–54; d'Alembert's dream discourse and, 144; body and, 150; strategies of, 173. *See also* Interference; Interruption; Noise; Ternary model of communication

Interference: communication through, 44–47, 53–54, 55, 61–62; seduction paradigm and, 162. *See also* Interruption

Internalization: detours from circuit and, 16–17, 27; *Préface-annexe* conspirators and, 17–27

Interruption, as message, 71–76

Irony, 19, 25–26, 30, 136–37

Irreversible text: Suzanne's narrative and, 66–71; urgency and, 76–78

Jacques le fataliste (Diderot): hostess's story in, 71–74; interruption as message in, 71–76; reader in, 74, 76–78, 170, 174; tale of Jacques's loves in, 74–76; dialogues in, 105; sense of urgency in, 172; critical literature on, 221n20

La Religieuse (Diderot), *see* Religieuse, La

Leibniz, Gottfried Wilhelm, 50–51, 62

Le Rêve de d'Alembert (Diderot), *see* Rêve de d'Alembert, Le

Logical inconsistencies, *see* Inconsistencies

Louis XV (king of France), 94, 223n18

Loy, J. Robert, 84

Madin, Madame (character), 68–69; as "real" person, 14–15, 16, 22; role of, 14–16; death of Suzanne and, 21–22; wax seal incident and, 24

Materialist rhetoric, 137–38, 166, 173ff

May, Georges, 28–29, 36, 58, 65, 77f, 215n8, 217n12

Memoir-novel, 56–61

Mind-body distinction, 150. *See also* Body; Sensibility

Molecules, and sensibility, 135, 139, 157, 226n13

Montaigne, 101

Music: indirect communication and, 48–50, 51–54; Diderot's views on, 219n5

Musical conversation, 51–54, 61, 68, 71, 169

Mylne, Vivienne, 36, 220n14

Narrative structure: reader-text relation and, 58–61; absorptive text and, 69–71; disruption and, 74–76, 87–88, 103; present-past relation and, 97–98. *See also* Epistolary genre; Historical writing; Inconsistencies; Memoir-novel;

Ternary model of communication
Narrative temporality: author-reader relation and, 36; in *La Religieuse*, 63–65, 66–67, 220n16; in retrospective narration, 63–65; in Diderot's historical writings, 83, 94–98, 105–8, 114; traditional historical writing and, 85–86, 91; reversal of time and, 99–100; ternary circuits and, 112–14
Narrator-function, and reader-function, 70–71
Nature: disorder in, 3–5; causality and, 88–90; God and, 128–29; notion of sensibility and, 129; generative processes of, 136–39. *See also* Sensibility
Nero, 96
Noise: as necessary for communication, 6–7, 73–74; reader's involvement and, 55, 61–62, 78; vs. message, 75–76, 163; ternary relations and, 111; physiological effect of, 146–47, 149–50; for Serres vs. Diderot, 226n17. *See also* Interference; Interruption

Objectivity: in *Préface-annexe*, 20–27 *passim*; of reader of Richardson, 35–37

Performance: as communication, 43–44, 48–50; Suzanne's reaction to own, 50
Philosopher: harpsichord analogy and, 129–30, 131; transformation of impressions into sounds and, 129–30, 131, 133
Philosophical cabal, 116–19
Philosophy: Diderot's fiction and, 79; object of, 118; harpsichord-philosopher analogy and, 129–130, 131. *See also* Enlightenment philosophy; Leibniz; *Rêve de d'Alembert, Le*; Serres
Pincer, as term, 130–31
Political events, interpretation of, 115
Polyphony: in *Histoire*, 100f, 103; in *Essai*, 101–3, 224n21
Prayer, as indirect communication, 44–48, 50–51, 62, 68
Préface-annexe of *La Religieuse* (Diderot), 11–38; autograph manuscript of, 7–8, 29, 217n12; novelistic plot of, 12–18 *passim*, 28–29, 31; conspiratorial plot in, 14, 23, 26–27, 29–31; wax seal incident in, 22–25, 215n8; reader in, 25–27, 169; critical interpretation of, 27–33; "Question to Men of Letters" in, 34–35, 37; contagious affective states in, 171–172. *See also Religieuse, La*
Present-past relation: Diderot's historical writing and, 94–98, 99–100, 120, 223n12; narrative strategy and, 97–98. *See also* Chronological order; Narrative temporality; Time
Prigogine, Ilya, 4

Rameau, Jean Philippe, *Castor et Pollux*, 49, 50
Raynal, Abbé, 84–86. *See also Histoire des Deux Indes*
Reader: perspective of, 25–27; destabilization of position of, 33–38, 107–8, 116; active involvement of, 53–54, 55, 61, 112–13, 116–18, 166; privileged access of, 53–54, 61; obstacles for, 54–55; narrative structure and, 88; recreation of experience and, 100; polyphony and, 102–4; discontinuities and, 103–4; dialogue with, 105–7; conventional historical writing and, 109–11, 115; as philosopher, 116–17, 118–19, 224n22; hostile, 119–20; Diderot's concern with posterity and, 120–23; points of insertion for, 162–63, 169–71, 172; contagious affective states and, 171–173. *See also under specific works*
Reader-author relation, 33–38, 69–71
Reader-function, and narrator-function, 70–71
Reader-text relation: as interactive, 58–61, 173–75; temporality and, 65, 68, 97–98; seduction of reader and, 76–78; inclusion-exclusion dynamic and, 163
Realism, 36–37
Reason, and sensibility, 151–54

Receptivity, and sensibility, 129
Religieuse, La (Diderot), 41–79; communication through interference in, 44–47, 53–54, 55, 61–62; ternary model and, 45, 61–63; reader in, 53–54, 55, 169; inconsistencies in, 56–60, 63–65, 66–67, 172, 219n10; as memoir-novel, 56–61; revisions to manuscript of, 58; reader-text relation in, 58–61, 65, 68; postscript in, 67–71; narrative strategy in, 69–71, 97–98; critical interpretation of, 172, 218n1. *See also Préface-annexe* of *La Religieuse*
Responsiveness, and sensibility, 130–31
Retrospective narration: destabilization of, 55–63; temporal model of, 63–71; classic, 65–66, 67, 219n8; reader-author relation in, 69–70; of Suzanne Simonin, 107
Rêve de d'Alembert, Le (Diderot): causality and, 89, 223n12; ternary model and, 127–28; sensibility in, 128–35; similarities between rhetorical structure and generative processes in, 140–45, 146–49; noise in, 146–47, 149–50, 163; seduction paradigm in, 156–60; reader in, 161–65, 169–70, 174; contagious affective

states and, 173; critical literature on, 224n1
Reversible time: in classic retrospective narration, 65–66, 67; in Suzanne's narrative, 66–71
Rousset, Jean, 216n10

St. Amand, Pierre, 221n22
Salon, eighteenth-century, 117–18
S'arranger (term), 225n8
Scientific theory: disorder in, 3–5
Secular, as term, 62
Secular genesis, 140
Seduction paradigm: female voice and, 25n; in *La Religieuse*, 70, 76, 174; Suzanne as reader and, 70; in *Rêve*, 156–60, 162–64, 165; points of insertion for reader and, 170–71
Seneca: Diderot's identification with, 95–98, 99–100, 121, 122–23; Diderot's differences with, 98–99; Diderot's rehabilitation of, 109–10, 111–12; role of, in Diderot's experience, 117–18
Sensation, as term, 131–32
Senses, 129
Sensibility: notion of, 128, 129–33; transformation from inert to active state of, 133–36, 137–38; as general quality of matter, 133–40, 225n9; communication of, 135, 154–56; communicative links and, 139–40; activation of, 141–45, 146–48, 153–54; reason and, 151–54; contagious quality of, 160–61; eating and, 225n10; symptoms of active, 226n15
Serres, Michel, 5–7, 50, 52–53, 78
Sexuality, 56–59, 220n12, 220n14, 227n19
Simonin, Suzanne (character): role of first letter by, 12–15; wax seal incident and, 22–24; social alienation of, 41–42; futility of direct communication and, 42–44, 48; musical conversation of, 51–54, 61, 68, 71, 169; role as narrator, 54–55, 171–72; suppression of knowledge by, 56–59, 64–65
Sleep, 143–45
Spider web metaphor, 148–49
Starobinski, Jean, 96, 224n20
Stewart, Philip, 65
Succession, and sensibility, 131–32
Suillius, 109–10, 123

Ternary model of communication: indirect communication and, 45; Leibnizian model and, 50–51; Serres model and, 52–53; destabilization of, 61–63; narrator as reader and, 69–71; participation of reader and, 104–8; variations of, in historical narrative, 108–21

passim; Diderot's opponents and, 121–22; reader's body and, 173
Time: complexity of experience of, 79; reversal of, 100; in generative processes, 138–39; in conversations of *Rêve*, 140–41, 145. *See also* Chronological order; Inconsistencies; Narrative temporality; Present-past relation

Uncertainty, 92
Undank, Jack, 215n6
Urgency, 76–78, 172
Ursule, Soeur (character), 42, 51–54, 61f, 169

Varloot, Jean, 214n1, 225n7
Volland, Sophie, 161
Voltaire, 88, 115–16

Wax seal incident, 22–25, 215n8

LIBRARY OF CONGRESS CATALOGING-IN-PUBLICATION DATA
De la Carrera, Rosalina.
    Success in circuit lies : Diderot's communicational practice / Rosalina de la Carrera.
        p.   cm.
    Includes bibliographical references and index.
    ISBN 0-8047-1923-3
    1. Diderot, Denis, 1713–1784 — Criticism and interpretation.
I. Title
PQ1979.D36   1991
848'.509 — dc20   91-2608
                                                                  CIP

♾ This book is printed on acid-free paper